A Handbook on

DEATH *and*

BEREAVEMENT (2)

Helping Children Understand

compiled by Desmond Spiers

REACH

National Advice Centre for Children with Reading Difficulties

Published by REACH:
National Advice Centre for Children with Reading Difficulties
California Country Park, Nine Mile Ride,
Finchampstead, Berkshire RG40 4HT

Produced by Signpost Books
Printed and bound in Great Britain by
Biddles Ltd, Guildford and King's Lynn

ISBN 0 948664 25 8

Cover illustration by Gregory Rogers from *Lucy's Bay* (entry number 84)
by Gary Crew and Gregory Rogers.
Reproduced by kind permission of Jam Roll Press, Queensland, 1992.

This handbook is published with the support of the Reader's Digest

CONTENTS

Introduction 5

How to use the Book List 11

Key to Abbreviations Used 11

The Book List 12

Author Index 65

Keyword Index 67

Organisations and their Addresses 69

INTRODUCTION

Six years ago REACH published *A Handbook on Death and Bereavement: Helping Children Understand;* in response to requests from two schools for appropriate material that would assist them in coping and coming to terms with tragic deaths in their own small communities. The success of this handbook, and the continuing requests for information on death and grieving from parents, teachers, librarians, health workers, social workers and community groups, convinced us that there is a need for a second handbook. There is also now a greater awareness of the devastating and sometimes misunderstood effect death will have on people, particularly children, that is reflected by the fact that most schools now include work on death and bereavement in Personal and Social Education (PSE) courses, and many have put together special bereavement boxes.

Attitudes to talking about death, especially with children, have undergone a significant change since 1992. The public reaction to the death of Diana, Princess of Wales in 1997, and Professor Robert Winston's groundbreaking 1998 BBC television documentary on the human body from birth to death, which actually showed a man dying, are very good examples of this more open attitude. We are constantly being exposed to natural and human disasters through newspaper, radio and television coverage. These events make us all aware of the fragility of human life, and as literature reflects reality, these horrifying and deeply affecting events become part of the literature that adults and children read.

The awareness that the reality of death cannot be hidden from children of any age, is reflected by the wider range of material available for pre-school and infant children in this handbook. When the mother of a five-year-old boy gave birth prematurely, resulting in the death of the baby, the family's health visitor contacted REACH for age appropriate books to help explain that not all babies are born alive. For many years the death of premature babies was shrouded in secrecy, with the body being removed and buried without the parents being allowed to see it. It is now recognised that it is important for the parents to be allowed to see and hold their child, and they are encouraged to name, grieve and bury the baby. Increasingly siblings are also being allowed to see and hold the dead baby. Children look forward to the arrival of a baby brother or sister, and when it does not happen, there are many questions as to 'why', as occurred in this case. In response to this enquiry *Remembering Michael* (105) was recommended.

The needs of children and adults who have learning problems and are grieving, are also being recognised and more material is being written for their use, either on their own or for sharing with another person. As an indication of the openness now associated with special needs education, a public library contacted REACH looking for age and ability appropriate material for a teenage boy with cerebral palsy and learning problems, whose older brother had committed suicide. A number of titles were recommended for the teenager, along with support material for the parents and carers. The list included *When Something Terrible Happens: Children Can Learn to Cope with Grief* (143), a book that allows children to record their understanding about life before the tragedy occurred, how they feel now, and what they think will happen to them in the future.

Since the first handbook appeared, an increasing amount of space in professional literature is being devoted to the understanding of the specific needs of people who are facing their own death, the death of a loved one, are grieving, and who, in addition, have a learning problem, or emotional, sensory and physical difficulties. There are also publications to help the many parents suffering a form of grief when the baby they have been expecting is born with a disability or learning problem. In a similar way, if a child develops a learning problem or disability because of an accident or illness, the parents, siblings, other family members and friends grieve for the 'death' of the 'perfect' child they knew. *Dying and Disabled Children: Dealing with Loss and Grief* (37), covers this area with sympathy and understanding of the multitudinous feelings of grief and guilt felt by the family.

Some children and young adults with learning problems may find it difficult to communicate their emotions orally or in writing, especially when dealing with such an emotive issue as death and terminal illness, but the drawings children produce can provide an insight into their feelings, and their view of the world. A number of professional titles explore this area in some detail, for example *Drawings from a Dying Child: Insights into Death from a Jungian Perspective* (34), which analyses the drawings produced by seven-year-old Rachel, terminally ill with cancer. There is also a growing practice amongst social workers and therapists to encourage children and adults to construct a 'memory book' detailing their feelings about the bereavement and loss of a family member or friend. The *Memory Book* (90) produced by Barnardo's is an excellent example of how a simple task can help a child or adult come to terms with loss.

With the best of intentions, adults may still in many cases try to protect the child from the realities of illness and death; the younger the child the more often this happens. However, from a very early age children sense the emotions of the people around them, and worry about the unknown. The suspicion that they are being excluded, coupled with a lack of information can lead them to create a fantasy picture that is more frightening than the reality of the situation. Also the use of euphemisms such as 'he's gone to sleep', can be taken literally by children, leading to a fear that if they go to sleep they may die. Children respond to honesty and facts given at a level they will comprehend, backed up by a supportive relationship with parents, family and carers. Recently a clinical psychologist working with young children approached REACH for help in building a collection of material suitable to use with children aged four to six, who had parents, relatives or friends with life threatening conditions and illnesses. One of the titles suggested by REACH was *Losing Uncle Tim* (82) in which a young boy's favourite uncle is dying of AIDS.

Children quite often take upon themselves the blame and guilt for problems arising within a family, for example a separation or divorce. 'I didn't love daddy or mummy enough, if only I had done as they told me'. And after a disagreement children sometimes wish their parents were dead.

If a divorce, serious illness or death should occur soon afterwards, then this guilt factor may come to the fore and expand out of all proportion. Social workers contend with this constantly. In one case REACH was able to find appropriate material for use with three children - ages six to eleven -whose parents had separated. One of the children thought she was to blame for the separation. Then the father died suddenly and all three children were racked with guilt that they were the cause of his death. It was therefore important to find titles that would deal with this aspect of the children's grief, as well as the concrete issues surrounding the death. *Saying Goodbye to Daddy* (112), which includes this facet of guilt as part of the storyline, was thought to be appropriate.

Many children understand that death is something that occurs eventually, but assume that it only happens to old people, for example grandparents. Though shocked, most children will take such a death in their stride. But it is as difficult for children to accept the death of a parent or sibling, as it is for a parent to accept the death of a child. The effect on a family of the death of a child can be very traumatic. Not only does the family have to deal with the loss, but grief also affects the child's teacher and school, friends, community and religious groups. In fact anyone who has been even remotely connected with that child's life will be affected.

Whatever the death, it is now possible to prepare the child theoretically for such an eventuality. Talking about death in schools and at home will help, even though it is removed from their immediate experience. The use of books as bibliotherapy after the event can be useful, but it can also be too late - the worst has already happened. Knowing where to go for assistance ('Useful Organisations and their Addresses' – p69-72), combined with these two approaches is probably the most comprehensive and satisfactory method.

This handbook does not claim to be an exhaustive list of material on the subject, but it does provide a comprehensive range of titles. There are picture books for young children as well as for older children, and fiction titles for all age ranges, as well as reference material for children and adults.

Subjects covered include accidental death, violent death, and loss of a parent, grandparent or sibling. Caring for those with a terminal illness, their death, and the feelings of those left behind is explored in many of the titles. Books for adults about burial, cremation, and religious observances to help explain the many facets of death to children, are included. Because of the emotions they produce many of the titles are difficult to read.

Since the first handbook was written, much new material has been published on death and grieving, both factual and fictional, for professionals, families and children. And because of this we felt that it would not be possible to simply update the existing handbook, but to compile this new handbook to use along side the earlier edition. The majority of the 113 titles in *A Handbook on Death and Bereavement: Helping Children Understand* (pub. 1992) are still in print, and the handbook itself is available from REACH.

More than 250 titles, most of them published after 1992, have been read and assessed to select the 147 annotated titles that have been included in this handbook. The material has been selected to complement and expand on the coverage in the first handbook. Though the majority of the titles are British, material from Australia, Canada, New Zealand and the USA is included, thus widening and strengthening the range of viewpoints available on the subjects of death and grief.

All the editions available at the time of compilation are listed, including any large print, and non print formats we could trace. Therefore all titles (including any which have since gone out of print), should be available via your local school or public library services, or bookshops.

HOW TO USE THE BOOK LIST

All books are listed in alphabetical order by title with an entry number. An author index is included as is a keyword index. Against each keyword are the numbers of the entries that will apply to that particular topic. Some titles may be keyword indexed more than once. The Age Reading and Age Interest levels given are general guidelines and should not be taken as prescriptive. A list of organisations who offer help and advice to those caring for children who are suffering from a life-threatening condition, and people who have been bereaved and are grieving is included.

KEY TO ABBREVIATIONS USED

Hb - hardback

Pb - paperback

Lf - large format

Lp - large print

A SAMPLE ENTRY

92   MY BROTHER SAM IS DEAD
Collier, James Lincoln
Atlantic Books, 1974, ISBN 0 590 42792 X Pb
Cornerstone, USA, 1988, ISBN 1 55736 038 3 Hb, Lp
Age Interest: Yr.8-12   Age Reading: Yr.7+

Tim's brother Sam joins the American forces in the war against the British. As the fighting comes nearer and engulfs the small town in which the family lives, the horror of war and its effect on ordinary people is shown. Additionally the book shows how rational thinking disappears in war time. Tim's father disappears and finally Sam is unfairly court-martialed and executed. Although Sam and Tim and their family are fictitious, many of the other characters and events are real.

1   ABOUT DYING
   STEIN, Sara Bonnett
   FRANK, Dick
   Walker and Company, USA, 1974, ISBN 0 8027 7223 4 Pb
   Age Interest: Adult

A book for parents and children to share on dying and death. It includes two stories - one about the death of a pet bird, the other about the death of a grandfather. The right hand page has black-and-white photographs telling the story, while the left hand page has two sets of text - large bold text complementing the photographs for children to read, and smaller text for adults, giving helpful hints on what the child may be thinking/experiencing, as well as ideas to help the child understand what is happening. The author feels that trying to protect a child from dying and death can be more harmful than the truth. The child will know something is happening, and without the full story may build up a fantasy picture, which could be even more frightening.

2   AFTER CHARLOTTE'S MOM DIED
   SPELMAN, Cornelia
   FRIEDMAN, Judith
   Albert Whitman, USA, 1996, ISBN 0 8075 0196 4 Hb
   Age Interest: Yr.4 - Yr.6   Age Reading: Yr.3+

A picture book dealing with a six-year-old girl's attempts to come to terms with her mother's death six months previously in a car crash. Dad withdraws into himself not realising Charlotte's fears and confusions - particularly her fear of going to sleep, as she has been told her mum has gone to sleep. Dad's lack of communication leaves Charlotte isolated with her feelings, and matters come to a head after an outburst with her friends at school. Charlotte and dad go to see a therapist, and finally she is able to talk to her father about her fears and worries. A much better relationship develops between them, and on the last page Charlotte is able to laugh at something; a positive note on which to end.

3   AIDS IN THE FAMILY
   SPURRIER, Libby
   Hodder & Stoughton, 1994, ISBN 0 340 58973 6 Pb
   Age Interest: Adult

Families of sufferers, and people with AIDS talk about the disease, and how they have coped and adapted so that they can continue to lead as normal a life as possible. Parents and siblings are quite often the last to know, sometimes not being told until the sufferer has been HIV positive for a number of years. Apart from the trauma of adapting to this terminal illness, family members may also have to come to terms with the sexuality of the person with AIDS. For many families the disease is kept hidden because of the fear of alienation by relatives, friends and neighbours. A very poignant book that also contains practical information and details of support groups for those with AIDS and their families.

4   ALL IN THE END IS HARVEST:
AN ANTHOLOGY FOR THOSE WHO GRIEVE
WHITAKER, Agnes ed.
Darton, Longman & Todd, 1991, ISBN 0 232 51624 3 Pb
Age Interest: Adult

Written in conjunction with Cruse, a national organisation providing an information and support service for the bereaved, this book contains hundreds of poems and pieces of prose on the themes of death, grief and the meaning of life. Most of the items selected have been used by Cruse counsellors throughout the country, and have proved to be helpful to bereaved people. Eight chapters lead the reader through the different stages and different types of grief and mourning, and include material from other cultures and religions, for example the chapter 'Prayers from Many Sources'

5   ASPECTS OF GRIEF: BEREAVEMENT IN ADULT LIFE
LITTLEWOOD, Jane
Routledge, 1992, ISBN 0 415 02816 7 Pb
Age Interest: Adult

Death is a traumatic experience, and if it is the death of a partner or a child the impact can be devastating. In eight chapters Jane Littlewood looks at various aspects of death and the grieving process, and draws upon personal testimonies of those who have suffered a bereavement to illustrate how the grieving process progresses over a period of time, how one can help and what support is available. Chapters include: Rituals and Mourning Customs; Professional Support Networks; Informal Support Networks; Death of Children; and Death of Partners and Parents. This book will probably be of use to those whose work brings them into regular contact with people who are dying or are bereaved.

6 BADGER'S PARTING GIFTS

VARLEY, Susan

HarperCollins, 1992, ISBN 1 85681 164 6 Hb

Age Interest: Yr.1 - Yr.5   Age Reading: Yr.3+

Badger is old and knows he will soon die; he isn't afraid but is worried about the friends he will leave behind. He tries to prepare them by saying that he will soon be going down the 'Long Tunnel', but after his peaceful death his friends are very sad and unhappy. The author uses the cold of winter as an analogy for death, and when spring comes his friends start to remember all the happy memories they have of Badger, and slowly their sadness disappears. The natural stages of death and grieving are explained simply in this picture book with comforting illustrations.

7 BEYOND GRIEF: A GUIDE FOR RECOVERING FROM THE DEATH OF A LOVED ONE

STAUDACHER, Carol

Souvenir Press, 1988, ISBN 0 285 65068 8 Hb

Souvenir Press, 1988, ISBN 0 285 65069 6 Pb

New Harbinger Publications,1987, ISBN 0 934986 43 6 Pb

Age Interest: Adult

Grieving takes many forms and in some cases may not be recognised. The author, through her own experience of grief, reaches out in this book to those who are suffering to help them understand and come to terms with their feelings. Three sections: Understanding and Coping; Surviving Specific Types of Loss; and Getting and Giving Help, are divided into eleven chapters dealing with such topics as: The Grief Experience; Surviving the Loss of a Child; Surviving Loss During Childhood; Helping Those Who Grieve. Within each chapter, there are short readable sections addressing specific areas of death and bereavement. A book that can be dipped into in response to specific circumstances.

8 BEYOND THE HORIZON: A SEARCH FOR MEANING IN SUFFERING

SAUNDERS, Cicely

Darton, Longman & Todd, 1990, ISBN 0 232 51875 0 Pb

Age Interest: Adult

The author has been at the forefront of the modern Hospice movement for the past forty years, and is the founder of the St Christopher's Hospice. In this book she shares with us the prose and poetry that she has used with the dying and their families, to help them come to terms with their situation. Topics discussed include anger, suffering, being left behind, and carrying on. Some of the material is well known, but much will be new including contributions from patients Dame Cicely has worked with over the years. At the beginning of each section she explains why she has chosen each item. A useful book for those looking for ways to express their own feelings.

9   BEYOND THE RAINBOW
FRASER, Christine Marion
Lions, 1994, ISBN 0 00 674623 3 Pb
Age Interest: Yr.7 - Yr.9   Age Reading: Yr.7+

Set in Scotland, this is the story of Kirsty, a young girl fighting to overcome leukaemia. Family life is not good as dad is away in Aberdeen during the week working for an oil company. Arguments between her parents are common, and instead of bringing the family together Kirsty's illness seems to be making the situation worse. While in hospital she makes friends with Jean who also has cancer. Because of their common situation they are able to comfort and strengthen each other. It takes all of Kirsty's resolve to carry on when Jean dies, when she herself is at her lowest from the cancer treatment. Her treatment proves successful, and Kirsty and her family slowly pick up the pieces of normal life.

10   THE BOY IN THE BUBBLE
STRACHAN, Ian
Mammoth, 1994, ISBN 0 7497 1685 1 Hb
Age Interest: Yr.7 - Yr.11   Age Reading: Yr.7+

Sixteen-year-old Adam, who has just moved into the neighbourhood, has Severe Combined Immunodeficiency Disorder (SCID), which means that he has to stay in a large sterile airtight tent as any germ could kill him. His mother is very over protective and wary of Anne, who lives across the road, and her overtures of friendship to Adam. Through Anne he 'experiences' the world outside his bubble. When the chance comes for him to have a bone marrow transplant and try new experimental drugs that might allow him to lead a normal life outside the bubble, he takes it, even though the odds are stacked against him. For a few days after the operation everything seems to be going well, then his body starts to reject the new tissue and infections set in. Adam makes the decision to reject any more treatment, so that he can have a few days as a 'normal' person, even though this will lead to his death. As time passes after Adam's death, Anne realises that through him she has grown up and experienced more of life than she would have had she and Adam never met.

11   THE CAROUSEL

ROSENBERG, Liz
LaMARCHE, Jim
Orchard Books, 1996, ISBN 1 86039 213 X Hb
Orchard Books, 1997, ISBN 1 86039 336 5 Pb
Age Interest: Yr.4 - Yr.6   Age Reading: Yr.4+

The carousel in the park was always a special place for two sisters and their mother. One winter after their mother's death, the girls are walking through the park when they discover that the carousel horses have come to life. A magical journey ensues, in which the girls remember many happy things about their mum. They decide the reason the horses are wild is because the carousel is broken. They manage to mend it with the help of mum's toolbox - mum was always good at mending things. Then they calm the horses down by playing the tune mum used to play if they couldn't sleep. They arrive back home wet and tired at the same time as dad, who remembers with a smile that mum always used to say the park was magical in the rain. A positive book, with colourful atmospheric illustrations.

12   CHILDREN AND BEREAVEMENT

DUFFY, Wendy
Church House Publishing, 1995, ISBN 0 7151 4846 X Pb
Age Interest: Adult

Each year many thousands of children are affected by death and adults need to understand that they respond to death differently from adults. The author looks at how children of different ages view death, and how their grieving progresses through different stages. Chapters include: Terminal Illness; Sudden Death; Suicide; The Funeral. Through a clear understanding of the grief process in children, adults will be in a better position to make the appropriate responses. This short readable book filled with good common-sense information is a must for parents and those working with children who have been bereaved.

13   CHILDREN MOURNING, MOURNING CHILDREN

DOKA, Kenneth J. ed.
Taylor & Francis, 1995, ISBN 1 56032 447 3 Pb
Age Interest: Adult

Written in association with the Hospice Foundation of America, and arising out of a conference, this text explores in detail the grieving process in children. Three main themes are addressed: Children are always developing and so therefore is their understanding of death; Children grieve in ways that are different from and similar to adults; and Children need significant support as they deal with loss.

Additionally there is a section on 'The Child's Response to Life Threatening Illness'. Each section is subdivided into chapters written by a range of social workers, psychologists, gerontologists, and ministers of various religions. A comprehensive overview.

14   A CHILD'S QUESTIONS ABOUT DEATH
St. Catherine's Hospice, Crawley, W. Sussex, RH10 6BH, 1989
Age Interest: Yr.1 - Yr.6   Age Reading: Yr.4+

A short sixteen-page booklet for adults explaining in simple language the questions most frequently asked by children about death and dying - Where Do Dead People Go? Is Death Like Sleeping? How Long Will I Live? The text only takes up about half of each page, the rest being given over to simple illustrations.

15   CHINA'S PLUM TREE
STANLEY, Elizabeth
Freemantle Arts Centre Press, Australia, 1992, ISBN 1 86368 024 1 Pb
Age Interest: N - Yr.3   Age Reading: Yr.2+

This story about the death of Tom's cat China, is told in simple sentences with bold print and clear colour illustrations. Tom is very fond of China, but he is getting old, and after a visit to the vet he learns that the cat is going to die. Tom cherishes their remaining days together and China is buried under his favourite plum tree. Tom misses China and is lonely, but his grief is helped when dad brings home a new kitten. The new kitten will not replace China, but provides continuity of life.

16   THE CHRISTMAS MIRACLE OF JONATHAN TOOMEY
WOJCIECHOWSKI, Susan
LYNCH, P J
Walker Books, 1995, ISBN 0 7445 4007 0 Hb
Age Interest: Yr.4 - Yr.7   Age Reading: Yr.4+

Since the death of his wife and baby son, Jonathan Toomey has become so hard and cold that the village children call him Mr Gloomy. A new resident to the village, a widow, asks him to carve a nativity set for her son Thomas. Sometimes she and her son ask if they can watch quietly while he works. As each piece is carved a little part of Jonathan's heart unfreezes. He begins to talk to Thomas and slowly a relationship develops. Finally on Christmas morning as the figures of Mary and Baby Jesus are finished, he realises that there is life after the death of loved ones. A happy Jonathan goes to church with the widow and her son, and no one calls him Mr Gloomy again. A heart-warming story with rich, detailed colour illustrations.

17 COPING WITH SUICIDE: A PASTORAL AID
GREEN, Gerard
Columba Press, 1992, ISBN 1 85607 046 8 Pb
Age Interest: Adult

This book is written from the perspective of the teachings of the Roman Catholic Church by a practising priest as a guide to assist other priests in dealing with the suicide of a parishoner. It is divided into four main sections: Suicide and the church's teaching; Support for the family and friends bereaved; Advice and examples for a funeral; Grieving process after the funeral, with a special look at grieving in children. It is full of practical advice, some of which is applicable outside the Roman Catholic Church.

18 COPING WITH SUICIDE
SCOTT, Donald
Sheldon Press, 1989, ISBN 0 85969 585 9 Pb
Age Interest: Adult

Over the past decade there has been a steady increase in suicides, particularly amongst young people. The author looks first at some of the underlying reasons for suicide, and how the reader as a parent, teacher, sibling, friend, or relative may be able to spot some of the danger signs and take appropriate action, either alone or with professional help. The last part of the book takes the reader through the aftermath and grieving process if a suicide should occur. Suicide is still a taboo subject in many quarters, but this sympathetic book will hopefully make the topic better understood and a more approachable subject for discussion.

19 COT DEATHS: COPING WITH SUDDEN INFANT DEATH SYNDROME
LUBEN, Jacquelynn
NCVO Publications, 1989, rev ed. ISBN 0 7199 1264 4 Pb
Age Interest: Adult

Cot death is a very traumatic subject, which this book handles with delicacy and compassion, as the author herself lost a baby through cot death. Practical advice and information are presented in ten short accessible chapters, dealing with issues such as: A Tragedy Occurs; The First Week; Emotions and Reactions; The Next Pregnancy; Looking Back. Three appendices give information for doctors on helping parents who have lost a baby through cot death, and also a list of do's and don'ts for those who come into contact with the bereaved family.

20 DADDY'S CHAIR

LANTON, Sandy

Kuperard, 1995, ISBN 0 929371 51 8 Hb

Age Interest: Yr.1 - Yr.3   Age Reading: Yr.3+

After Michael's dad dies of cancer, he has difficulty in both understanding and coming to terms with the death. He is very protective of 'daddy's chair' and places a sign on it forbidding others to sit in it. The story is set within a Jewish family, and the book also explains in a sensitive way some of the rituals involved e.g. *Shiva*, the Jewish week of mourning, and is illustrated with unusual sepia-like drawings. Mum carefully explains and answers Michael's questions until in the end the chair becomes a special place where Michael can remember his dad and he is able to remove the sign.

21 DANCE ON MY GRAVE

CHAMBERS, Aidan

Bodley Head, 1992, ISBN 0 370 30366 0 Pb

Age Interest: Yr.9+   Age Reading: Yr.8+

This is a novel for older children, as it deals with two subjects that in some quarters are still regarded as taboo: namely death and a gay relationship between the two main characters. Hal's boat capsizes while he is out sailing at the beginning of the summer holidays after finishing his exams. Rescued by 18-year-old Barry, he falls in love and they spend an idyllic summer together. When Barry dies in a motorcycle crash, Hal is bereft and has a breakdown, leading him to desecrate Barry's grave. The story is told in the present tense, through diary recollections and newspaper cuttings. It is not an easy book to read because of the subject matter and prose style, but is one which would lend itself to group discussion.

22 THE DARK CARD

EHRLICH, Amy

Walker Books, 1991, ISBN 0 7445 3021 0 Pb

Age Interest: Yr.7 - Yr.10   Age Reading: Yr.8+

Seventeen-year-old Laura is looking for a means of escape from the reality of the death of her mother. She feels isolated and her father does not seem interested in her sorrow. Living in Atlantic City, the gambling mecca of the east coast of America, she starts to frequent the casinos and there meets and makes friends with a number of people. By observing their lives, and their hidden secrets, she comes to a better understanding of her own life - namely that her happiness lies in her own hands.

23 THE DARK UNCERTAINTY: WRESTLING WITH SUFFERING AND DEATH

CLARK, David and Sarah
Darton, Longman & Todd, 1993, ISBN 0 232 51976 5 Pb
Age Interest: Adult

One of a series of books in a series entitled 'The Wounded Pilgrim', that explores the link between psychological pain and spiritual growth. This title explores the premise that apart from death, other aspects of life such as illness, loss of hope and mental illness, can cause grief and suffering. The authors examine the many facets of grief and suffering from the Christian viewpoint, and discuss how suffering and death can focus an individual's thoughts on whether God exists, and the meaning of life. They include personal testimonies from people they have worked with, to substantiate some of the arguments and proposals included in the book.

24 DEAD: THE STORY OF DEATH AND DYING

HATFIELD, Jim
Franklin Watts, 1993, ISBN 0 7496 1186 3 Hb
Franklin Watts, 1994, ISBN 0 7496 1596 6 Pb
Age Interest: Yr.4 - Yr.9   Age Reading: Yr.5+

A title from the factual 'Horrible Histories' series, that includes all the interesting bits children enjoy reading about, but which most books usually leave out. For interesting, read strange, odd, fascinating and slightly gruesome. The main facts are given in a straightforward manner, interspersed with cartoons giving more obscure information. For example, in the chapter 'Testing For Death' there is a graphic cartoon with the fact 'The Romans would chop off a finger to see if it bled'. Each section is a two-page spread, covering topics such as: Testing for Death; Embalming; Burial; Grave Goods; Life after Death.

25 DEATH

BRYANT-MOLE, Karen
Wayland, 1995, ISBN 0 7502 0398 6 Hb
Wayland, 1994, ISBN 0 7502 1379 5 Pb
Age Interest: Yr.4 - Yr.9   Age Reading: Yr.5+

A title in the 'What's Happening?' series. Each two page spread looks at a different aspect of death and grieving. Topics include: When Do People Die; Is It My Fault; The Funeral; What Happened; The Future. In addition there is a chapter for parents and teachers with suggestions on how to use and share the book with children. There is also a short glossary explaining some of the special words associated with death. The text is written simply and is complemented by colour photographs of children and adults. A good introduction to an emotive subject for upper primary children.

26   DEATH AND BEREAVEMENT
The Chalkface Project, PO Box 907, Milton Keynes MK5 6BR, 1995, ISBN 1 873562 98 5 Pb
Age Interest: Adult

A teaching pack to use with children of mixed ability to explore the themes of loss, dying, death and grieving. Though probably of more use within the secondary school, some sections would be of help to primary school teachers. Twenty eight topics dealing with death are explored within a double-page spread. On the left-hand page are notes for the teacher, while the right-hand page contains a worksheet for the pupils. All the student sheets are photocopiable. Issues looked at include: Life Cycle; Ideas About Death; Talk to Me; Bottling It Up; After a Death.

27   DEATH CUSTOMS
RUSHTON, Lucy
Wayland, 1992, ISBN 0 7502 0419 2 Hb
Age Interest: Yr.3 - Yr.9   Age Reading Yr.4+

Each culture and religion has its own beliefs about what happens to people when they die. This book in the 'Understanding Religions' series looks at death customs and the principles behind them, and explores the way Buddhists, Christians, Hindus, Jews, Moslems and Sikhs deal with death. Each topic is looked at in general, and then from the viewpoint of each religion. Topics include: Being Ready to Die; Burial and Cremation; Mourning; Remembering. A very straightforward book that is accessible to children.

28 DEATH AND LOSS: COMPASSIONATE APPROACHES IN THE CLASSROOM
LEAMAN, Oliver
Cassell, 1995, ISBN 0 304 33087 6 Hb
Cassell, 1995, ISBN 0 304 33089 2 Pb
Age Interest: Adult

A title in the 'Studies in Pastoral Care and Personal and Social Education' series, which looks at issues of current and continuing concern. The books are written by teachers and educationalists combining both theory and practical examples. This title arose out of a need for a book to help teachers and schools cope when a death or impending death occurs within the school. The author visited many schools around the country to find out the strategies they used in dealing with death. From his research Mr Leaman puts forwards ideas and suggestions which are not prescriptive, so that teachers and schools can formulate a programme to use within PSE.

29 DEATH IN THE CLASSROOM
GATLIFFE, Eleanor D.
Epworth Press, 1988, ISBN 0 7162 0441 X Pb
Age Interest: Adult

Originally written by a teacher who had difficulty finding appropriate material on the subject, this ten-year-old book is still relevant, and will be of use to teachers wishing to explore the issues of death and dying with their students within a classroom situation. The book is set out in such a way that teachers can use it to plan a series of lessons as part of the curriculum within either PSE or Religious Education. Religious and non-religious viewpoints on death are examined.

30 DEATH IN THE FAMILY
RICHARDSON, Jean
Lion Publishing, 1993, 2nd ed. ISBN 0 7324 0628 5 Pb
Age Interest: Adult

Drawing on first-hand experience and written from a Christian perspective, this guide will help anyone who has to deal with death within the family. It is a very readable book divided into thirteen chapters. Subjects covered include: Understanding Death; Different Types of Bereavement; What Will It Mean; The One Parent Family, Earning a Living. Throughout the book the needs of children are addressed, and in addition there is a chapter dealing specifically with children and how they react to death at different ages.

31 DEATH IS NOTHING AT ALL

HOLLAND, Canon Henry Scott
SAUNDERS, Paul
Souvenir Press, 1987, ISBN 0 285 62824 0 Hb
Age Interest: Yr.4+   Age Reading: Yr.3+

These well-known words have been used at countless funerals over the years. This time they have been published in a small illustrated book.

32 DOG'S JOURNEY

KEMP, Gene
HOWARD, Paul
HarperCollins, 1996, ISBN 0 00 675137 7 Pb
Age Interest: Yr.4 - Yr.6   Age Reading: Yr.3+

Widget and her little brother Tim move to a house in Devon. There are new friends to be made and the countryside to explore with their dogs Russet and Dizzy Frizzy. Life seems perfect as summer turns into autumn, but tragedy imposes when Russet is knocked down and killed by a car. Widget is devastated and blames her mum for Russet's death, but a harsh winter sees her learning that life does continue. The book is produced as a paperback with a fairly simple text, divided into short chapters with numerous black-and-white illustrations.

33 DOLPHIN BOY BLUE

ARENA, Felice
HarperCollins, 1996, ISBN 0 00 675198 9 Pb
Age Interest: Yr.7 - Yr.9   Age Reading: Yr.6+

Micky's father has not allowed him to go out on boats since his mother Mary was drowned ten years previously, and he was mysteriously saved by a dolphin. Now on his thirteenth birthday the dolphin reappears, and starts 'communicating' with him, leading Micky to reassess his and his father's feelings over his mother's death, and in particular the boating restriction his father has placed on him. Running parallel to this story are Micky's endeavours at a national swimming competition and his feelings for the girl who has lived next door all his life. The dolphin acts as a catharsis for Micky and his father to finally accept the death and get on with their lives.

34 DRAWINGS FROM A DYING CHILD: INSIGHTS INTO DEATH FROM A JUNGIAN PERSPECTIVE

BERTOIA, Judi
Routledge, 1993, ISBN 0 415 07218 2 Hb
Routledge, 1993, ISBN 0 415 07219 0 Pb
Age Interest: Adult

The drawings children produce can provide an insight into their feelings on a whole range of issues, and a view of the world as they perceive it. Professionals working with children use this method of obtaining information, especially from younger children who may not have the vocabulary to explain how they are feeling. This book analyses the drawings produced by Rachel, terminally ill with leukaemia between the ages of seven and nine. Through her drawings, with analysis and explanations from the author, we follow the course of the illness, Rachel's fears, anger, awareness that she was dying, and acceptance of her impending death. This book provides many insights into how children perceive dying and death, and includes practical strategies to assist families and those caring for children with a terminal condition.

35 DREAMSPEAKER

HUBERT, Cam
General Paperbacks, Canada, 1989, ISBN 0 7736 7230 3 Pb
Age Interest: Yr.10+   Age Reading: Yr.9+

This is an uncompromising book to read. It follows the story of Peter, an eleven-year-old boy who has been emotionally damaged from years of being passed from foster home to foster home, and eventually to an institution for delinquent boys. Pursued by nightmares, he escapes into the forests of British Columbia and meets an old Indian, the Dreamspeaker of the title, and his companion a mute man who has also been physically and emotionally damaged. With the friendship and love of the two Indians, Peter slowly starts to face his fears and realise that he has it within himself to overcome them. Additionally, through his own damaged soul, he is able to reach out to the mute Indian. Peter's first 'real' home and chance of happiness is destroyed when he is found by the authorities and taken back to the institution. Though in the end Peter's suicide is inevitable, it still comes as a shock, as does the rest of the explosive conclusion. The print is exceedingly small.

36 DYING
HINTON, John
Penguin, 1972, 2nd ed. ISBN 0 14 013060 8 Pb
Age Interest: Adult

The author is a psychiatrist who has worked extensively with people suffering from terminal illnesses. This book examines the feelings and experiences of those faced with death, as well as their families and friends, and is divided into four main sections: Attitudes to Death; The Dying; Care of the Dying; Mourning. Each section is divided into chapters, as the author looks at specific areas, for example: Speaking of Death with the Dying; Awareness and Denial; Reactions to Bereavement. A very straightforward book, though the print is on the small side.

37 DYING AND DISABLED CHILDREN: DEALING WITH LOSS AND GRIEF
DICK, Harold M. et al
The Haworth Press, 1989, ISBN 0 86656 759 3 Hb
Age Interest: Adult

This book looks specifically at children with disabilities and how their condition can lead to grieving in the widest sense of the word by parents and family members, because their child is not 'perfect'. There are sections looking at amputation, chronic loss and disability, and life threatening diseases, as well as death. Within each section there are individual chapters written by experts in that particular field. This is a very specialised book looking at issues that are usually only touched upon in more general books on disability, death and bereavement. It is probably a book for the professional rather than parents.

38 EASEFUL DEATH: CARING FOR DYING AND BEREAVED PEOPLE
KATZ, Jeanne & SIDELL, Moyra
Hodder & Stoughton, 1994, ISBN 0 340 59514 0 Pb
Age Interest: Adult

The authors make extensive use of case studies that reflect our multi-cultural society to illustrate the needs of dying people. This is very much a book for nurses, social workers and carers working permanently or on a regular basis with people who are dying, and is full of practical information and suggestions. A large part of the book looks at the support required by the families and friends of the dying person both before and after the death. They are the people who have to continue with their lives after the death of a loved one.

39 THE EMPTY BED: BEREAVEMENT AND THE LOSS OF LOVE
WALLBANK, Susan
Darton, Longman & Todd, 1992, ISBN 0 232 51853 X Pb
Age Interest: Adult

The author has extensive knowledge of death and bereavement, having worked for Cruse since 1978 and written numerous articles on the subject. In this book she looks at an area of death that is frequently ignored or lightly touched upon in other books; namely, the repercussions of losing a sexual partner. In the second of the six chapters this book contains, she examines 'Different Love - Different Loss' looking at amongst others Young Love; Cohabitation; Homosexual Partners, Lovers; Young Widow/Widower and how family, friends and society react to the death of the partner and the person left behind. Each bereaved person has their own set of problems and the author examines some of these and gives encouragement and advice on how to survive and face the future.

**40 ENDURING SHARING LOVING: FOR ALL
THOSE AFFECTED BY THE DEATH OF A CHILD**
SHAWE, Marilyn
Darton, Longman & Todd Ltd, 1992, ISBN 0 232 52010 0 Pb
Age Interest: Adult

An anthology of poetry and prose aimed at bereaved parents written by people trying to make sense out of the death of a child. It is divided into three sections: Enduring the Pain looks at the reactions to such a death, with all the associated emotions of disbelief, shock, anger and despair. Sharing the Loss explores the needs of bereaved adults and children to talk about what has happened. The final section Loving Our Children celebrates the uniqueness of children and the joy they bring to our lives. The author hopes that the anthology will assist in the grieving process.

41 EXPLAINING DEATH TO CHILDREN
GROLLMAN, Earl A. ed.
Beacon Press, USA, 1969, ISBN 0 8070 2385 X Pb
Age Interest: Adult

This book was one of the first comprehensive studies compiled on the subject of death and its effect on children, and is as relevant today as it was when it was first published thirty years ago. Earl Grollman has written many books on death, but here edits ten essays by American experts in the fields of child guidance, psychiatry, psychology, religion and sociology. Topics discussed include: How Younger Children View Death and Themselves; The Child and Death as seen in Different Cultures; Children's Books Relating to Death: A Discussion. It is very much a book for the professional or student studying the subject.

42 FLIP-FLOP GIRL

PATERSON, Katherine
Gollancz, 1994, ISBN 0 575 05776 9 Hb
Puffin, 1996, ISBN 0 14 037591 0 Pb
Age Interest: Yr.5 - Yr.7   Age Reading: Yr.5+

Set in small-town America where, following the death of their father, Vinnie, her brother Mason and their mother move from the city to the country to stay with Grandma. Vinnie has trouble fitting in, especially as Mason has become mute since dad's funeral. An unlikely friendship develops with another girl, Lupe, (who wears flip-flops), which helps Vinnie overcome her grief. Written by the author of *Bridge to Terabithia*, it is a touching but funny story, written in fairly complex language and divided into short chapters without illustrations.

43 THE FLOWER KING

HOWARTH, Lesley
Walker Books, 1995, ISBN 0 7445 3190 X Pb
Age Interest: Yr.8 - Yr.12   Age Reading: Yr.8+

The narrator of this story sees people and everyday events in colour - red is *danger*, black is a *cruising shark*, green is *feelgood*, blue is *calm* and *neutral*. On his regular Saturday visit to see his great uncle in the local nursing home, he befriends another resident, Mrs Pinder. Through her he comes to the know the history of the village and in particular the 'Flower King', who grew acres of flowers for the local markets when Mrs Pinder was a girl. As the tragic story of the 'Flower King' unfolds it has a lasting effect on the narrator and all those around him.

44 FOGHORN PASSAGE

LOHANS, Alison
Stoddart, Canada, 1992, ISBN 0 7737 5496 2 Pb
Age Interest: Yr.8 - Yr.12   Age Reading: Yr.7+

Matt is involved in a car accident that kills his sister and leaves him a paraplegic. Sammie, who is an acquaintance in the youth orchestra, is still mourning the death of her father from cancer. Matt is very depressed and doesn't see any point in living, Sammie isn't sure why she wants to help him as he can be so obnoxious, but a tentative friendship does start, and over the course of a year they are able to help each other come to terms with the changes in their lives. Set in British Columbia.

45   THE FORGOTTEN MOURNERS: GUIDELINES
FOR WORKING WITH BEREAVED CHILDREN
PENNELS, Sister Margaret, SMITH, Susan C.
Jessica Kingsley Publishers, 1996, ISBN 1 85302 264 0 Pb
Age Interest: Adult

Sixty pages of concise pertinent information and advice aimed primarily at teachers and social workers, who work with bereaved children. Short clearly laid out chapters are rounded off by a list of key points which should prove useful as an aide memoir. Chapter 1 - How Children Grieve looks at the grieving process at different ages, and this is followed in the next chapter by clear guidelines and suggestions on the appropriate language that should be used. The remaining five chapters continue in the same practical vein. Finally, two appendices give links to other relevant resources.

46   FRED
SIMMONDS, Posy
Puffin, 1989, ISBN 0 14 050965 8 Pb
Age Interest: N - Yr.5   Age Reading: Yr.2+

The story of Fred the cat is told in a light-hearted comic strip format. Fred has died of old age, and Nick and Sophie will miss him even though he was a lazy old cat. They bury him in the garden alongside a guinea pig and rabbit, previous pets that died. That night the two children are woken by the noise of all the other cats, Fred's friends, celebrating his life. They go down and join in. Next morning the whole family is surprised to discover a gravestone has appeared in the garden to 'Famous Fred'.

47   THE FRIENDS
GUY, Rosa
Gollancz, 1974, ISBN 0 575 01839 9 Hb
Puffin, 1994, ISBN 0 14 037177 X Pb
Age Interest: Yr.7 - Yr.10   Age Reading: Yr.7+

Set in New York, this is the story of Phyllisia, who with her sister and parents has moved from the West Indies to America. She is finding it very difficult to settle in her new neighbourhood and school, with the added complication that her mother is terminally ill. Phyllisia does not want to think about her mother's impending death. She forms an unlikely friendship with Edith who is a bit of a miscreant, with a totally different view of life. And it is with Edith's help that Phyllisia slowly settles in to life in New York, and comes to terms with her mother's eventual death.

48   GOING BACKWARDS

KLEIN, Norma

Scholastic, USA, 1986, ISBN 0 590 40328 1 Hb

Age Interest: Yr.8 - Yr.12   Age Reading Yr.7+

Sixteen-year-old Charles doesn't have much self esteem, he's not very successful with girls, his younger brother is a much better musician, and he and his mother don't get on very well. When his grandmother Gustel, who is suffering from the onset of Alzheimer's disease comes to live with the family, it is another burden he has to bear. This Gustel is not the grandmother he remembers who played tennis with him, went hunting for shells, who was full of life. The author has captured the pain that Alzheimer's causes not only to the person concerned but also to their family. Eventually they cannot cope with grandmother anymore and it is decided that she will have to go into a home. However, before this happens Gustel dies and Charles has to contend with another set of emotions.

49   GOOD-BYE, CHICKEN LITTLE

BYARS, Betsy

Heinemann, 1993, ISBN 0 435 12406 4 Pb

Age Interest: Yr.4 - Yr.7   Age Reading: Yr.5+

Jimmy Little is constantly embarrassed by the eccentricities and reckless behaviour of his family. When Uncle Pete decides to walk across the wide frozen river in the town, Jimmy is horrified but there is nothing he can do to stop him. Tragically the ice breaks and Uncle Pete drowns. Jimmy feels guilty that he didn't try harder to stop his uncle, and in his time of need it is his eccentric family that helps him come to terms with his uncle's death.

50   GOODBYE PAPPA

LEAVY, Una

EACHUS, Jennifer

Orchard Books, 1996, ISBN 1 85213 713 4 Hb

Age Interest: N - Yr.3   Age Reading: Yr.2+

When Shane and Peter go to stay with their grandfather they collect mushrooms and hen's eggs, help in the garden, and late at night listen to him playing his accordion. After their visit and return home, pappa suddenly dies. They return for the funeral and when they are frightened by their feelings, mum suggests they think of all the happy times they had together. The text is in short understated sentences with detailed illustrations.

51 GRANDMA'S BILL

WADDELL, Martin
JOHNSON, Jane
Macdonald, 1995, ISBN 0 7500 0307 3 Pb
Macdonald, 1998, ISBN 0 7500 2627 8 Pb Lf
Age Interest: N - Yr.3   Age Reading: Yr.2+

One day when Bill goes to tea with grandma he notices a photograph of his grandad, also called Bill. Grandma gets out the family photograph album and explains each picture to him. He discovers a lot about his dead grandfather and the rest of his family too. He also learns something about the sense of security and continuity a family gives, and a feeling for his place within it. The text is simple and clear and the illustrations are a clever mixture of colour, with black-and-white for the family photographs.

52 GRANDMOTHER

HUBNER, Franz
HOCKER, Kirsten
Neugebauer Press, 1992, ISBN 1 85618 031 X Hb
Age Interest: N - Yr.5   Age Reading: Yr.2+

A delightful picture book telling the story of Tommy and his wonderful Grandmother Marie and the great times they have together. However, one day Grandma Marie tell Tommy that she is dying and that she will be dead by the time Tommy's favourite flower in the garden dies. Tommy thinks that if he can keep the flower alive then Grandma will also live. Sadly both the flower and grandma die. However the next spring the flower blooms again, and Tommy learns that life carries on.

53 GREEN WILLOW'S SECRET

DUNLOP, Eileen
Puffin, 1995, ISBN 0 14 036907 4 Pb
Age Interest: Yr.8 - Yr.10   Age Reading: Yr.7+

Kit's sister Juliet is dead, and the family move from Edinburgh to part of a large house in the country. Kit is adopted, and in addition to feeling relieved she no longer has to compete with Juliet, she also feels that perhaps she should have been the one to die. At a loose end, she starts to explore the house and the grounds that are full of Japanese objects, and discovers a Japanese garden, where she is sure she sees a ghost. Meeting Daniel, a boy who lives close by, they start to track down the mystery of the garden and house and come into contact with the old lady who owns the property. Secrets hidden from the turn of the century start to emerge. By exploring another family's problems Kit begins to have a better understanding of her own family.

54 GRIEF COUNSELLING AND GRIEF THERAPY: A HANDBOOK FOR THE MENTAL HEALTH PRACTITIONER

WORDEN, J William
Routledge, 1991, 2nd ed. ISBN 0 415 07179 8 Pb
Age Interest: Adult

This is an updated and expanded version of a classic text on the subject of grief counselling for those working in this specialised field. Two chapters deal with normal grief reactions and facilitating uncomplicated grief; abnormal grief reactions and resolving pathological grief, and another chapter looks at special types of loss through, for example, suicide, AIDS, miscarriage and sudden death. One section looks at grief within the family. There is a comprehensive bibliography.

55 GRIEF, DYING AND DEATH: CLINICAL INTERVENTIONS FOR CAREGIVERS

RANDO, Therese
Research Press, USA, 1984, ISBN 0 87822 232 4 Pb
Age Interest: Adult

For those working with the terminally ill and dying, in particular professional carers, the constant exposure to death can present difficulties as it confronts them with their own mortality. Dr Rando begins this book by examining our own attitudes to death, explaining that only by looking at these fears and feelings can we understand what a patient is feeling and be better able to assist them. Apart from her own professional expertise as a clinical psychologist, the author has drawn upon the knowledge of others who have worked with terminally ill people in the USA from the mid 1960's. This is a very comprehensive book, which is more suitable for the professional.

56 A GRIEF OBSERVED

LEWIS, C. S.
Faber & Faber, 1966, ISBN 0 571 06624 0 Pb
Age Interest: Yr. 10+   Age Reading: Yr. 10+

C S Lewis wrote this book following the death of his wife. It is a very touching account of one person's response to grief and his attempt to understand his feelings at the death of a loved one. He is able to convey what most people who have been bereaved feel but lack the ability to express.

57   GRIEVING AFTER THE DEATH OF YOUR BABY
KOHNER, Nancy
Professional Care Productions,
1 Millside, Riversdale, Bourne End, Bucks. SL8 5EB,
1993, Pb
Age Interest: Adult

A short supportive and practical publication to help anyone whose baby has died. Part One is a collection of stories from parents who have lost a baby. Though they can be harrowing to read, many parents find they are helpful, as they show they are not alone in the memories and feelings they have.   Part Two examines ways of grieving and gives ideas and suggestions to help - these include memory boxes (a box full of momentos of the dead baby). There is a companion video called *When Our Baby Died*, which is reviewed later in this handbook (141).

58   A GUIDE FOR CARERS AND OTHER PROFESSIONALS
CATHCART, Fiona
British Institute of Learning Disabilities, 1994,
ISBN 1873791 26 7 Pb
Age Interest: Adult

This is the third of three booklets in the series 'Understanding Death and Dying'. The series is aimed at adults with learning problems, their families and professionals working with them. There is much in each book that will also be of relevance and use to children with learning problems and those assisting them to comprehend and come to terms with the death of a family member, friend or pet. It breaks the subject matter down into simple concepts and ideas to ease the transferral of the ideas and information to the person concerned. The other two booklets are also reviewed (59 & 147).

59   A GUIDE FOR FAMILIES AND FRIENDS
CATHCART, Fiona
British Institute of Learning Disabilities, 1994,
ISBN 1 873791 21 6 Pb
Age Interest: Yr.10+   Age Reading: Yr.9+

This is the second of three booklets in the series 'Understanding Death and Dying'. The series is aimed at adults with learning problems, their families and professionals working with them. There is much in each book that will also be of relevance and use to children with learning problems and those assisting them. In this book ideas and guidelines are given so that families or friends can assist someone who has a learning problem understand what death is, what will happen to the dead person, and emotions the bereaved may be feeling. There is also a short chapter on the death of people who have learning problems and the effect it has on family and friends. The other two booklets are reviewed (58 & 147).

60 HEAVEN

ALLAN, Nicholas

Hutchinson, 1996, ISBN 0 09 176537 4 Hb

Age Interest: Yr.1 - Yr.6   Age Reading: Yr.2+

Most children at some point will ask 'What is heaven like?' This picture book is about Dill the dog who tells his owner Lily that he is going to heaven. Lily wants to go too, but Dill says it's not time for her. They then have a conversation as to what heaven will be like; Lily thinks it will be never-ending fairground rides and ice-cream; Dill says it will be bones, lampposts and wiffy things on the ground. Lily then says 'Anyway, you might not go up - you might go DOWN'. Dill replies 'But I've always been a good dog ... All right, I've tried to be good dog'. A very simple but philosophical picture book on death

61 HELEN THE FISH

KROLL, Virginia

WEIDNER, Teri

Albert Whitman, USA, 1992, ISBN 0 8075 3194 4 Hb

Age Interest: N - Yr.3   Age Reading: YR.3+

The complete story about owning a pet, from beginning to end. Hannah is only three when her big brother Seth gives her a goldfish for her birthday. He helps her with all her problems, like giving it a name, feeding it, and looking after it. Time passes, Hannah grows bigger and goes to school. Then one day she comes home to find Helen floating upside down in the tank. Once again Seth helps her through her problems, this time in dealing with her grief. Things finally get back to normal, and in the end they buy another goldfish, but this time as a present for someone else (a twist in the tail!).

**62   THE HELPER'S JOURNEY: WORKING WITH PEOPLE
FACING GRIEF, LOSS, AND LIFE-THREATENING ILLNESS**
LARSON, Dale G.
Research Press, USA, 1993, ISBN 0 87822 344 4 Pb
Age Interest: Adult

Divided into three parts: Exploring the Inner World of Helping, The Interpersonal
Challenge, and Creating Caring Systems - this book explores the many facets of
being a carer to those who are dying and their families. Part One examines what a
carer is, how they can improve their understanding of the patients feelings and
most importantly manage the stress that is involved in being a carer. The second
section looks in more detail at the relationship carers have with their patients and
the communication skills that are required to be an effective helper. Finally, as most
carers work as a part of a team, the book examines what makes for good team work
and the balance between individual and team responsibilities.

63   HELPING CHILDREN COPE WITH SEPARATION AND LOSS
JEWETT, Claudia
Free Association Books, 1994, 2nd ed. ISBN 0 7134 7766 0 Pb
Age Interest: Adult

Children can experience loss in many ways through separation, divorce, and moving
away from familiar surroundings as well as through death. In this updated edition
the author, a child and family therapist, explores all these aspects of loss. Topics
include: Telling Children about Loss; Helping Children Face Change;
Understanding and Supporting Grief; Facilitating the Grief Process; Looking Back,
Letting Go, and Moving On.   She describes the techniques, illustrated by case
histories, she has developed over many years of working with children, including
sample dialogues. The book will assist adults working with children who are
grieving for whatever reason.

64   HIDDEN LOSS: MISCARRIAGE AND ECTOPIC PREGNANCY
HEY, Valerie et al
Women's Press, 1996, 2nd ed. ISBN 0 7043 4457 2 Pb
Age Interest: Adult

The four authors state 'Why is the reality of prebirth loss hidden under euphemism
and evasion? Why can it be so difficult for us to grieve?' Written from a feminist
viewpoint, this title analyses how the experience of miscarriage is viewed in modern
society. Part One looks at first-hand accounts from a number of women. Part Two
explores feminist issues, Part Three looks at medical viewpoints and the final
section examines how women come through such a traumatic experience and carry

on with their lives. Full of practical information, the authors address a difficult topic with sensitivity.

65   I CARRIED YOU ON EAGLES' WINGS
MAYFIELD, Sue
Scholastic Children's Books, 1995, ISBN 0 590 55939 7 Pb
Age Interest: Yr.7 - Yr.11   Age Reading: YR.7+

With his mother dying of leukaemia, fifteen-year-old Tony tries to show a brave face to the world, but sometimes it becomes too much and he wishes he could just fly away. Because his father is a minister, many people seem to assume that Tony has extra resources to cope with pain and grief, but he doesn't. Finding and looking after a seagull with a broken wing, which he eventually releases back to the wild, helps him accept that he has to let his mum go as well. A second book entitled *A Time to be Born* reviewed later in this handbook (127), follows Tony after his mother has died.

66   I DON'T KNOW WHAT TO SAY...: HOW TO HELP
AND SUPPORT SOMEONE WHO IS DYING
BUCKMAN, Dr. Robert
Pan, 1996, ISBN 0 330 34754 3 Pb
Age Interest: Adult

In many cases most of the care of a dying person will be carried out either by the medical professon, or the immediate family and friends. This book includes much practical information and advice for people in such a situation. Thirteen chapters deal with such topics as: Sensitive Listening; Being Ill; The Last Stage; Saying Goodbye; Talking With Health Professionals. This is a very readable book grounded in practicalities rather than theory.

67   I HEARD THE OWL CALL MY NAME
CRAVEN, Margaret
Picador,1980, ISBN 0 330 24765 4 Pb
Age Interest: Yr.8+ Age Reading: YR.8+

The haunting story of a young Anglican priest, who does not realise he is dying, and has only two or three years to live. He is sent by his Bishop to a small Indian village in the wilds of British Columbia, where the Bishop hopes Mark will prepare for the time when he is informed of his impending death. Living and experiencing the seasons in this wild landscape, along with the villagers' joys and sadness, he learns much about life and is able to accept his own impending death with equanimity.

68 I MUST TELL YOU SOMETHING: ROSEMYN'S STORY ABOUT THE SUDDEN DEATH OF HER MOTHER

BO, Arno

Bloomsbury Children's Books, 1996, ISBN 0 7475 2514 5 Pb

Age Interest: Yr.5 - Yr.8   Age Reading: Yr.5+

Nine-year-old Rosemyn recounts the true story of the car accident that she, her sister Phoebe and mum and dad were involved in, followed by their stay in hospital. All of them have been badly injured, particularly mum, who sadly dies. Rosemyn's story is very powerful and honest and captures the feelings of a nine-year-old girl perfectly. The book is written in diary-form, with a daily entry from the day of the accident until about three weeks later, which is when she comes home from hospital, after the funeral.

69 I NEVER TOLD HER I LOVED HER

CHICK, Sandra

Livewire, 1989, ISBN 0 7043 4912 4 Pb

Age Interest: Yr.8 - Yr.12   Age Reading: Yr.7+

How often has a child told a parent in a fit of anger that they wished they were dead? Now that Frankie's mum is dead, she would like to take back these and all the other horrible things she said. As the elder sister she is now 'expected' to be mother to her younger brother. She tries to come to terms with her own emotions, but isn't very sure what feelings she is supposed to have. Frankie also has to contend with her father's emotions, as they swing backwards and forwards. However, the three of them slowly start to come to terms with mum's death.

70 I'M A VEGETARIAN

LEACH, Bernadette

Attic Press, Eire, 1992, ISBN 1 85594 040 X Pb

Age Interest: Yr.8 - Yr.11   Age Reading: Yr.7+

Thirteen-year-old Vanessa is finding it difficult to cope with the death of her father. However, her mother has decided that the best thing for them to do is to move and start afresh. The chosen place is Cork in southern Ireland, where mum has obtained a job lecturing in English Literature. Vanessa is horrified, but there is nothing that she can do to change her mum's mind. Big brother Ed who is in his last year of A Levels is staying behind living with an uncle, and will not be there for support. The move is made, and we follow Vanessa as she commences a new life which is filled with some surprising, funny, and sad moments.

71 IN THE SPRINGTIME OF THE YEAR

HILL, Susan

Penguin, 1977, ISBN 0 14 004110 9 Pb

Age Interest: Yr.11+   Age Reading: Yr.10+

The author has drawn on her own personal experience of losing a loved one in this novel. We follow Ruth as she mourns and tries to come to terms with the loss of her husband Ben. Set in the Oxfordshire countryside earlier in this century it evocatively portrays the ebb and flow of the seasons which reflect Ruth's grief.

72 A JEWISH BOOK OF COMFORT

KAY, Alan A

Kuperard/Jason Aronson, 1995, ISBN 0 87668 589 0 Hb

Age Interest: Adult

As the United Kingdom is a multi-cultural society, there is a need for material that examines how beliefs other than Christianity, view and deal with death, mourning and bereavement. Interspersed throughout this step-by-step guide to the traditions, rituals and rules of Jewish mourning are readings and thoughts - Jewish and non-Jewish - that the author found of comfort after his father died.

73 JOHN'S BOOK

FULLER, Jill

TOOP, Bill

Lutterworth Press, 1993, ISBN 0 7188 2870 4 Hb

Age Interest: Yr.5 - Yr.7   Age Reading: YR.4+

John's father dies suddenly of a heart attack during the school holidays, and he takes on the mantle of looking after his mum. He will be the man of the house. John tells the story of the funeral, going back to school, first birthdays and Christmas without dad. He eventually realises that he cannot replace his father. When his mother meets and falls in love with a new man, other hurdles have to be overcome. John is helped by his aunt who puts together a special book containing his family tree and old photographs. From this he is able to accept the changes and his new family. The story is told in some detail, in small print with a few black and white drawings.

74 JUST ONE TEAR

MAHON, Kate
FEDDERSEN, Melanie
Angus & Robertson, Australia, 1992 ISBN 0 207 17454 7 Pb
Age Interest: Yr.6 - Yr.10   Age Reading: Yr.6+

This is a most perceptive novel written by a fourteen-year-old girl in response to the death of the father of one of her friends. Written in diary form we follow a thirteen-year-old boy as he tries to understand his feelings and emotions after his father is shot and fatally wounded. As the only witness, he also has to contend with the trial of his father's murderer. Narrated in short sentences, packed with emotional punch, this book gets right inside the head of a child grieving for the loss of a parent.

75 KAREN'S GOLDFISH

MARTIN, Ann M.
TANG, Susan
Scholastic, 1994, ISBN 0 590 55441 7 Pb
Age Interest: Yr.3 - Yr.5   Age Reading: Yr.3+

This is a title in the 'Babysitters' series. Mum and dad have divorced, and seven-year-old Karen and her little brother Andrew have each been given a goldfish to have as a pet when they stay with their dad and his new wife. Karen calls her fish Crystal Light, but sadly it dies. Karen displays anger and grief at her loss, but holding a funeral for the fish, assisted by her friends, helps her accept it. Finally she is able to replace Crystal with another goldfish.

76 THE KITE AND CAITLIN

McGOUGH, Roger
PRATER, John
Bodley Head, 1996, ISBN 0 370 32371 8 Hb
Age Interest: Yr.2 - Yr.6   Age Reading: Yr.3+

Caitlin has been very ill for the past two years, in and out of hospital. She is now home, very weak and unable to walk. Mum buys a kite for her brother Jack, which he does not want, but Caitlin does. She feels the kite is sad to be earthbound like her, and that one day it will fly high. Summer comes and Caitlin dies. The kite takes her higher than the highest mountain to a place where she will never be in pain and where happiness awaits her. This is a very tender book dealing with a sensitive subject - the death of a child.

77 LEARNING TO SAY GOODBYE: DEALING WITH DEATH AND DYING

PECK, Rosalie & STEFANICS, Charlotte
Taylor & Francis, 1987, ISBN 0 915202 71 9 Pb
Age Interest: Adult

We will all encounter death at some point in our lives. When it happens why is it so hard to say 'goodbye', particularly when a parent is involved? Religions round the world teach that after dying we go to a better place, but this still doesn't stop us trying to put off the inevitable. The authors examine these natural emotions, and look at ways in which we can come to accept and understand them, and by doing so be in a better position to face up to our own mortality.

78 LIFE AFTER LIFE: READINGS AND PRAYERS TO COMFORT THE BEREAVED

SMITH, Fraser
Society for Promoting Christian Knowledge, 1993,
ISBN 0 281 04718 9 Pb
Age Interest: Adult

The author, a minister, compiled this book of readings, quotations and prayers in response to requests from mourners for copies of the words he had used during funeral services. He has gathered his material from a wide range of cultures and beliefs around the world. All the writings share one thing in common, giving comfort, encouragement and hope to carry on. A very useful book for those planning or looking for appropriate words to say at a funeral or memorial service.

79 LITTLE OBIE AND THE FLOOD

WADDELL, Martin
LENNOX, Elsie
Walker Books, 1991, ISBN 0 7445 1768 0 Pb
Walker Books, 1997, ISBN 0 7445 5449 7 Pb
Age Interest: Yr.3 - Yr.5   Age Reading: Yr.3+

Set in the American West, probably in the late 1800s, the first of these four short stories tells of the flood that destroys the cabin belonging to Little Obie and his grandparents, and kills the parents of Marty, Obie's best friend. The next three tales follow Little Obie and Marty as they come to terms with the loss in their lives and sudden change, in particular the new family grouping with Marty living with Obie and his grandparents. Though simply written, the stories capture beautifully the sense of loss and bewilderment that has befallen the two children.

80   LIVING WHEN A LOVED ONE HAS DIED
GROLLMAN, Earl A
Souvenir Press, 1996, 2nd ed. ISBN 0 285 63319 8 Pb
Age Interest: Adult

With simple, short, but succinct words and sentences, the author takes the reader through what he sees as four stages in bereavement: Shock; Suffering; Recovery; A New Life. This book is not just for those who have suffered a bereavement, but also for family and friends who wish to comfort and help the person concerned. Earl A Grollman has written many books on death and bereavement, and is a well-known counsellor in America.

81   LOOKING FOR ATLANTIS
THOMPSON, Colin
Julia MacRae, 1993, ISBN 1 85681 266 9 Hb
Red Fox, 1996, ISBN 0 09 964521 1 Pb
Age Interest: Yr.5 - Yr.10   Age Reading: Yr.5+

The pages of this picture book are full of the most fantastically intricate and fascinating pictures taking a boy, the hero of the story, on a journey of discovery. Recently the boy's grandfather had died and left him a treasure chest showing the way to Atlantis. The boy's search for Atlantis is eventually rewarded when he realises that though his grandfather may be dead, he is still with him through his hopes and dreams not only in his head but more importantly in his heart.

82   LOSING UNCLE TIM
JORDAN, MaryKate
FRIEDMAN, Judith
Albert Whitman, USA, 1989, ISBN 0 8075 4756 5 Hb
Age Interest: Yr.4 - Yr.7   Age Reading: Yr.4+

Daniel spends a lot of time with his Uncle Tim and notices that lately he has been getting tired very quickly. When Daniel asks his mum what is wrong, she tells him that Uncle Tim has AIDS and is dying. Daniel is distraught at this news, but carries on visiting his uncle. At one point he is worried that he could catch AIDS, but his parents explain that you can't catch AIDS just by being in the same room with someone, having a meal with them or hugging them. When Uncle Tim dies, he leaves Daniel some special things in his will, and he is able to look to the future. The story is told in fairly simple text with large colour pictures on each page.

83   LOSS AND CHANGE
MARRIS, Peter
Routledge, 1986, rev ed. ISBN 0 415 09862 9 Pb
Age Interest: Adult

The synopsis of the book states: 'Peter Marris shows how understanding grief can help us to understand processes of change, both personal and social, and to handle them with more compassion for ourselves and others.' He examines not only grief through death, but also the grief that occurs, for example, when families are split by divorce, or by the destruction of close neighbourhoods through urban renewal. This is not a book giving practical advice, but is more theoretical examining the 'psychological and social processes which underlie and complicate change' and would probably be suitable for students.

84   LUCY'S BAY
CREW, Gary
ROGERS, Gregory
Jamroll Press, Australia, 1992, ISBN 1 875491 08 2 Hb
Age Interest: Yr.6 - Yr.10   Age Reading: Yr.5+

A picture book with superb illustrations that will appeal to young adults. Sam spends many holidays at his grandfather's hut by the sea, but does not like the nights, as they bring back painful memories of the time he was in charge of his sister Lucy and she drowned. His parents and grandfather have told him of the memorial they left for Lucy in the bay where she drowned, but he has never been able to visit the spot. Finally, many years later, the day comes when he summons the courage to go back to the spot around the headland and is able to come to terms with her death.

85   THE MAN WHO WANTED TO LIVE FOREVER
HASTINGS, Selina
CARTWRIGHT, Reg
Walker Books, 1991, ISBN 0 7445 2077 0 Pb
Age Interest: Yr.3 - Yr.6   Age Reading; Yr.4+

A fairytale illustrating that no one can live for ever no matter how hard they try. Bodkin is a young man full of life and wants to stay that way for eternity. Setting out on a journey to find the secret to eternal life, he finally reaches the old man of the mountain who tells him that they can live as long as the mountain stands. So Bodkin moves into the man's mountain home. Many hundred years later Bodkin feels the need to visit the village where he had been born. The old man tries to stop him, but Bodkin is determined. However, 'Death' is waiting for him.

86 THE MEANINGS OF DEATH
BOWKER, John
Cambridge University Press, 1993, ISBN 0 521 44773 9 Pb
Age Interest: Adult

The author examines death and people's responses and reactions from the viewpoints of Judaism, Christianity, Islam, Hinduism and Buddhism - making it an invaluable tool for comparison. He looks at the underlying and sometimes hidden message that religious teaching gives, especially where it relates to life after death. Additionally he draws comparisons between the secular and religious views of death, and tries to show that they are probably closer together than most people assume and that they can support and complement each other. A book which delves into the philosophy of death, bereavement and mourning.

87 MEET THE AUSTINS
L'ENGLE, Madeleine
Lion, 1988, ISBN 0 7459 1385 7 Pb
Age Interest: Yr.6 - Yr.9   Age Reading: Yr.6+

The Austin family - two parents, two boys and two girls - live a life firmly rooted in their Christian faith. However, they are put to the test when they take in Maggie Hamilton who recently has been orphaned. Though they try to be understanding of Maggie's sorrow, the children in particular find her difficult to live with. Some of her behaviour and actions are unacceptable, but she thinks that she can do anything and the family will accept that it is a reaction to the death of her parents. She is finally brought up short, though in a gentle way, and made to understand that although death is tragic, life goes on.

88 MEGGIE'S MAGIC
DEAN, Anna
STEVENS, Colin
Viking, 1993, ISBN 0 670 82761 4 Hb
Age Interest: N - Yr.3   Age Reading: Yr.2+

Meggie was eight years old when she died and the family's grief is seen through the eyes of her younger sister. When she feels lonely and sad she decides to visit their 'secret place'. She is filled with memories and feelings of the times they shared together, especially their fantasy games like dancing for the queen and catching fairies in spider webs. Meggie may be dead but not her magic. A sensitive and uplifting story told quite simply, in short sentences with bright colourful illustrations.

89 MEMORY

MAHY, Margaret

Dent, 1993, ISBN 0 460 06269 7 Hb

Puffin, 1995, ISBN 0 14 037304 7 Pb

Age Interest: Yr.9 - Yr.11   Age Reading: Yr.8+

Two stories are interwoven in this book - that of nineteen-year-old Jonny who is mourning his sister who died in tragic circumstances and Sophie, an old lady with Senile Dementia. While searching for his sister's best friend Jonny meets Sophie West, and trying to escape from reality he moves in with her. As their lives intertwine Jonny learns valuable lessons in life. This story is set in New Zealand and the views on death and old age of both Maori and white cultures are explored.

90 MEMORY BOOK

O'BRINE, Rory & LINDSAY-SMITH, Carol

Barnardo's, 1995, loose leaf

Age Interest: N+   Age Reading Yr.1+

A set of A4 cards with guidance notes, on which someone who may be dying can record thoughts and memories for those who will be left behind. Alternatively the set can be used by the bereaved to record their thoughts about the person who has departed. They would be useful for children who want to record family memories from a terminally ill parent.

91 MOLLY'S ROSEBUSH

COHN, Janice

OWENS, Gail

Albert Whitman, USA, 1994, ISBN 0 8075 5213 5 Hb

Age Interest: Yr.4 - Yr.5   Age Reading: Yr.3+

Molly's mum is pregnant, and she is looking forward to being a big sister. One day on returning home from school her parents tell her the sad news that mum has had a miscarriage and the baby won't be born. Her parents, along with granny, explain that not every baby is born, all eggs don't hatch or buds flower. Molly and her parents plant a rosebush in memory of the baby. The simple text blends into the large colour illustrations on each page. The book contains a four-page introduction for parents with advice on dealing with and telling children about a miscarriage.

92   MY BROTHER SAM IS DEAD
Collier, James Lincoln
Atlantic Books, 1974, ISBN 0 590 42792 X Pb
Cornerstone, USA, 1988, ISBN 1 55736 038 3 Hb, Lp
Age Interest: Yr.8-12   Age Reading: Yr.7+

Tim's brother Sam joins the American forces in the war against the British. As the fighting comes nearer and engulfs the small town in which the family lives, the horror of war and its effect on ordinary people is shown. Additionally the book shows how rational thinking disappears in war time. Tim's father disappears and finally Sam is unfairly court-martialed and executed. Although Sam and Tim and their family are fictitious, many of the other characters and events are real.

93   MY DANIEL
CONRAD, Pam
Puffin, 1993, ISBN 0 14 036379 3 Pb
Age Interest: Yr.6 -Yr.9 Age Reading: Yr.6+

This is the story of Ellie and Stevie's Great Uncle Daniel and his search for dinosaur bones on their grandparents farm in Nebraska. It is set around the 1880s when many new dinosaur discoveries were being made in America. As they walk through the natural history museum in their home town, Grandma Julia tells them the story of her and Daniel's childhood in Nebraska and the adventures they got up to, along with Daniel's fascination with fossils. Not all the fossil hunters were digging for scientific knowledge, and many only wanted to make money as museums were competing to buy dinosaur bones. As they near the Dinosaur Hall Grandma's tale of Daniel's greatest discovery, and his tragic death at fifteen, comes to an end and they see his greatest discovery - a brontosaurus in all its glory. The author brings Daniel's story vividly to life,.

94   MY GRANDAD
ISHERWOOD, Sheila
ISHERWOOD, Kate
OUP, 1996, ISBN 0 19 272150 X Hb
Age Interest: Yr.1 - Yr.3   Age Reading: Yr.3+

A little girl's grandad has died, and this book is about her happy and special times with him. She has many memories, mostly quite ordinary, like going for picnics, shopping, gardening, shelling peas together, and including her best birthday present ever, her pet rabbit, which give the story wide appeal. It is both gentle and positive, and shows how memories can help to cope with sadness. It is presented in a structured and secure format of one page of short text, with a large soft-focus colour illustration on the facing page.

95 NORTHERN LIGHTS: THE SOCCER TRAILS

KUSUGAK, Michael Arvaarluk
KRYKORKA, Vladyana
Annick Press, Canada, 1993, ISBN 1 55037 339 0 Hb
Annick Press, Canada, 1993, ISBN 1 55037 338 2 Pb
Age Interest: Yr.4 - Yr.7   Age Reading Yr.4+

An Inuit tale of the after life. Kataujaq, a small Inuit girl, lives with her mother, father and grandmother. She learns many things from her mother but then a terrible sickness comes that affects many people. Mother is taken away in an aeroplane and Kataujaq never sees her again. Now Kataujaq says she is a big girl, but still misses her mother. One of the favourite pastimes of her village is to play football in the early winter. Sometimes the Northern Lights or 'Aqsalijaat' in Inuit can be seen. One evening when Kataujaq is feeling very sad and lonely, Grandmother tells her the story of how the Northern Lights came to be. She explains that when people die, their souls leave their bodies and go to heaven. They still love to play football and on clear moonlit nights they come out to play and all the thousands of people who have died are the northern lights chasing each other round the celestial football pitch.

96 ODETTE: A SPRINGTIME IN PARIS

FENDER, Kay
DUMAS, Philippe
Plexus, 1989, ISBN 0 906008 34 4 Pb
Age Interest: Yr.2 - Yr.5   Age Reading: Yr.3+

The last bird to be born is pushed out of the nest by her older siblings and falls down onto the straw hat of an old man who makes his living busking around the Paris metro. The old man takes the bird home, takes care of her and calls her Odette. They become good companions and Odette helps the old man by singing along to his accordion. Spring and summer pass and Autumn arrives. All the other birds fly south for the winter and the old man knows Odette must go or she will die. When Odette returns the next spring she goes in search of the old man, but he has died. However, he has left his straw hat in a tree by their favourite spot. She uses it for her nest and teaches her chicks the songs the old man used to play.

97   ON DEATH AND DYING

KUBLER-ROSS, Elisabeth

Prentice Hall & IBD, 1997, ISBN 0 684 84223 8 Hb

Routledge, 1989, ISBN 0 415 04015 9 Pb

Age Interest: Adult

After nearly thirty years in print this book is still one of the classic texts on how we approach and react to death and dying, whether in a professional or personal capacity. The author, a doctor, looks firstly at our fear of, and attitudes to, death and dying. She then examines in individual chapters what she sees as five stages of bereavement: Denial and Isolation; Anger; Bargaining; Depression; and Acceptance. The book arose out of her work with terminally ill patients, and in the main addresses issues on death where the person concerned, family and friends can plan for the eventual happening, rather than unexpected deaths.

98   THE ONE WHO CAME BACK

MAZZIO, Joann

Houghton Mifflin, USA, 1992, ISBN 0 395 59506 1 Hb

Age Interest: Yr.7 - Yr.10   Age Reading: Yr.7+

Alex and Eddie (both fifteen) live in a trailer park, are best friends and like to lark around the local mountain to escape the reality of their lives, particularly Eddie who has an abusive step-father. One day they decide to miss school and go to the mountain. However, as the sun sets Eddie wants one more game of hide and seek. When Alex can't find him he assumes Eddie is playing a joke and goes home without him. Back at the trailer park Eddie has not returned and Alex starts to worry. Eventually the police are called in and a search is carried out on the mountain but there is no trace of Eddie. The authorities cannot decide if Eddie has run away, or worse that Alex killed him. The mental anguish of Alex is vividly portrayed as he is propelled into the realities and pressure of the adult world. Eventually Eddie's body is discovered and his death is found to be accidental.

99   OPHELIA'S SHADOW THEATRE

ENDE, Michael

HECHELMANN, Friedrich

Thienemann, 1989, ISBN 3 522 47040 0 Pb

Age Interest: Yr.6+   Age Reading Yr.7+

Miss Ophelia always wanted to be a famous actress, but her voice was not loud enough so she ended up becoming the prompter. She enjoys her life in the theatre and learns all the great plays off by heart. Sadly times changed and the theatre closes. On the last night before she goes home she sees a lonely shadow who has no person to attach to and takes him in. Gradually other lonely shadows hear about Miss Ophelia, flock to her and are taken in. When she loses her home her shadow family decide they have to help her and decide to perform all the plays that she has taught them over the years. Miss Ophelia's Shadow Theatre becomes famous. One night driving to another venue they are caught in a blizzard and another shadow comes to Ophelia. This time it is death. She takes him in and is carried up to heaven. The final ending is more than a just reward for all of Ophelia's kindness. The illustrations that complement the text are wonderful.

100 THE OTHER SIDE OF MIDNIGHT
JORDAN, Sherryl
POLLARD, Bryan
Scholastic, 1993, ISBN 1 86943 043 3 Hb
Age Interest: Yr.3 - Yr.6   Age Reading Yr.4+

The parents of ten-year-old Jessie and her little brother Joel have died in the plague. Jessie slowly comes to terms with their death, but Joel still grieves for them. She tries everything she can think of to cheer him up; however nothing works. Finally she takes him to see Midnight, a woman who has special healing powers. Leaving Joel with Midnight, she is told to return in four days. When Midnight and Joel disappear and it is suggested that Midnight might be a witch, she goes looking for them. Jessie eventually finds out that the truth is not always as straight forward as it seems. Set in the Middle Ages.

101 PARENTAL LOSS OF A CHILD
RANDO, Therese A. ed.
Research Press Company, USA, 1986, ISBN 0 87822 281 2 Pb
Age Interest: Adult

Though all deaths are sad, the grief of losing a child can be particularly severe and long term, 'with major and unparalleled symptom fluctuations over time'. This book 'investigates this specific and quite unique case of bereavement'. The six sections are divided into thirty-seven different chapters written by a wide range of American authors, all of whom have an interest in or work in the field of thanatological literature (the study of phenomena and practices relating to death). Topics dealt with include: Guilt in Bereaved Parents, Stillbirth, Accidental Death, Suicide, Death of an Adult Child, Missing Children, Grief of Siblings, Family Therapy. The editor of this book states that 'The purpose of this book is to acquaint professionals in all disciplines with the experience of parental loss. Its goal is to promote more appropriate clinical interventions and therapeutic support for bereaved parents, while at the same time establishing more realistic expectations for coping with this particular loss.'

102 PIRATE THE SEAL
JOBLING, Brenda
Scholastic, 1996, ISBN 0 590 13501 5 Pb
Age Interest: Yr.5 - Yr.7   Age Reading Yr.4+

Ever since his mum died Ryan has been very lonely. His dad seems to have no interest in, or time for, him and there are no other children of his age on the island where they live. He makes friends with a young seal he calls Pirate because of the dark patch round one eye. This special friendship helps heal some of his loneliness. When Pirate is in danger and Ryan is also in trouble trying to save him, he finds out just how much his dad is missing his wife, and that he also has problems coping.

103 PLAY NIMROD FOR HIM
URE, Jean
Bodley Head, 1990, ISBN 0 370 31184 1 Pb
Age Interest: Yr.9+   Age Reading: Yr.8+

Christopher and Nick have been friends for most of their lives, in fact they are the only friends each other has. It is them against the world and they create a make-believe world where they become Oliver and Guy. Sometimes it is difficult to tell the difference between their real selves and their alter egos. Life is comfortable for the two of them until Sal appears on the scene and Christopher starts seeing there is life outside Nick's friendship. Nick is devastated and tries to win Chris back, eventually commiting suicide and trying to kill Christopher as well.

104 THE PROMISE
WESTALL, Robert
Thomas Nelson, 1990, ISBN 0 17 432339 5 Hb
Piper, 1991, ISBN 0 330 31741 5 Pb
Age Interest: Yr.7 - Yr.9   Age Reading Yr.7+

A tale of the supernatural. Bob falls in love with Valerie and is so besotted that he promises he will do anything she wants. When Valerie dies she comes back to haunt him, pleading that he keep his promise, and rescue her from death. An interesting tale of young love and the power of emotions.

105 REMEMBERING MICHAEL

HARPER, *Anita*

AVERLEY, *Helen*

SANDS, 28 Portland Place, London W1N 4DE, 1994,

ISBN 1 869903 21 8 Pb

Age Interest: Yr.4 - Yr.7   Age Reading: Yr.4+

Mum is in hospital having the new baby, but dad comes home to tell David and Sally that the baby was dead when it was born. The children want to know why, and dad says the doctors don't know why. The next day they go to visit mum in hospital, and are able to hold their baby brother, whom they decide to call Michael. Next comes the preparation for, and the actual funeral. The story is told mostly from David's viewpoint and though he tries to understand, he thinks that his feelings are not as important as his parents. He feels ignored and is angry, and school is difficult too. Time passes with little improvement in his feelings, so David phones his aunt to tell her how he feels. Mum overhears and matters come to a head; from then on the situation gradually improves. Michael becomes part of the family even though he had been with them such a short time. This is quite a detailed story with lots of dialogue and plenty of realistic colour pictures. Published by the Stillbirth and Neonatal Death Society.

106 REMEMBERING MY BROTHER

PERKINS, *Ginny*

MORRIS, *Leon*

A & C Black, 1996, ISBN 0 7136 4541 5 Hb

Age Interest: N - Yr.6   Age Reading: Yr2+

Told in photographs this is the story of Greg remembering his older brother Chris who died in 1993. We follow him, his other two brothers, sister and parents as they carry on their lives, interspersed by moments when they recall family events they shared with Chris. They go to Whipsnade Zoo for the first time since Chris died and have a wonderful day and Greg remembers some of the things he had done with Chris. At school we see the special tree Chris's friends planted after he died. Chris's grave is shown and Greg says his dad finds comfort visiting it, bringing flowers and tending it. This is a wonderful book to share with children who have lost a sibling.

107 RHYTHM AND BLUES

BAILEY, Ann

Faber & Faber, 1993, ISBN 0 571 16839 6 Pb

Age Interest: Yr.8 - Yr.11   Age Reading: Yr.7+

Matti, a keen drummer, lives with her widowed father and is exasperated by his new found religious fervour after years of being the wild man including spells in prison. As part of putting his life in order dad invites his two daughters by another women to come and live with them. This is too much for Matti to handle and she starts to goad her father. Matters come to head when she learns that Tessa, one of her half-sisters, is dying. Matti wonders what she has done to merit first the death of her mother, and now the impending death of her new-found half-sister. Extended families, hidden secrets, a bad relationship between a father and daughter and death are all explored in this novel.

108 A RIGHT TO DIE

WALKER, Richard

Franklin Watts, 1996, ISBN 0 7496 2412 4 Hb

Age Interest: Yr.6 - Yr.13   Age Reading: Yr.7+

This is aimed at a secondary school audience. The nonjudgemental text is interspersed with quotes from individuals, organisations and religious groups giving a wide range of viewpoints on issues such as Suicide, Euthanasia, Living Wills, Cryogenics. As discussions on death are becoming more open, especially in schools, this book will be an excellent starting point to explore many facets of an emotive issue. A title from the 'Viewpoints' series, which looks at topical issues.

109 A RING OF ENDLESS LIGHT

L'ENGLE, Madeleine

Lion Publishing, 1988, ISBN 0 7459 1383 0 Pb

Age Interest: Yr.7 - Yr.10   Age Reading: Yr.7+

Sixteen-year-old Vicky has never experienced death at close quarters before, but the death of a close family friend, who is the same age as her father, brings the realisation that death can strike anyone at any age. Additionally, she has to come to terms with the impending demise of her beloved grandfather who has leukaemia. She is left wondering if she will ever be happy again, but though tragic, the events of the summer show her that life carries on and happiness can still be found.

110 RIVER BOY
BOWLER, Tim
Oxford University Press, 1997, ISBN 0 19 271756 1 Pb
Age Interest: Yr.7 - Yr.11   Age Reading: Yr.8+

Grandpa is dying, and Jess and her parents take him back to his childhood home, so that he can complete his last painting, which is entitled 'River Boy'. For Jess, this will be her first experience of death. As she supports her grandfather in finishing his picture, she comes to realise the symbolism between the river's journey, and the life of her grandfather. A very poignant story and perceptive insight into a teenager's understanding of death. The 1997 Carnegie Medal winner.

111 THE SADDEST TIME
SIMON, Norma
ROGERS, Jacqueline
Albert Whitman, USA, 1986, ISBN 0 8075 7203 9 Hb
Age Interest: Yr.4 - Yr.6   Age Reading: Yr.3+

Three contrasting short stories about death to help explain to children how death occurs for different reasons. In the first story Michael's Uncle Joe dies after a long illness. Michael is worried that the same thing may happen to his parents. They explain that most people don't die young and that they are strong and healthy. The second story deals with the death of a child, an eight-year-old boy, who is knocked off his bike by a car and killed. The children in his class remember the good and bad times they had with him. Teddy was too young to die, it was an accident. The final story looks at a grandparent's death. There is still a lot of sadness, but after a long life death is part of the natural process. Each story is linked with a few words of explanation and there are black-and-white illustrations on almost every page.

112 SAYING GOODBYE TO DADDY
VIGNA, Judith
Albert Whitman, USA, 1991, ISBN 0 8075 7253 5 Hb
Age Interest: Yr.1 - Yr.4   Age Reading: Yr3+

Clare's father is killed in a car crash and this is a full account of the events that follow. Everything is covered in detail, almost a day-by-day record of exactly what happens and how the family feels and copes with everything. There is a page of simple text with a colour illustration on the facing page, including simple explanations of what a casket (coffin) is like and pictures of the funeral service. Although this book deals with feelings as well, it may be helpful in giving a clear explanation to young children about the burial process.

113 SAYING GOODBYE TO YOUR BABY
ALDERSON, Priscilla
SANDS, 28 Portland Place, London W1N 4DE, 1986,
ISBN 1 869903 00 5 Pb
Age Interest: Adult

The Stillbirth and Neonatal Death Society has written this short, accessible, informative and supportive twenty-six page booklet for parents whose baby has died before, during, or shortly after birth. It is also of use to professionals, family members and friends. Contents include: Naming your Baby, Keepsakes, The Autopsy, Anniversaries.

114 SECRET FLOWERS: MOURNING AND
THE ADAPTATION TO LOSS
JONES, Mary
Women's Press, 1996, ISBN 0 7043 4505 6 Pb
Age Interest: Adult

A personal testimony by the author written after her husband Stanley died of cancer. We follow her from the day Stanley was diagnosed as having an inoperable tumour with only a short time to live, through his time in a hospice, to arranging the funeral. The majority of the book is taken up with coping, and coming to terms with life after the funeral. She talks us through all the types of grief and anger that she felt, her good times and bad times. Though she will always miss him, there is life after the death of a loved one.

115 SEE YA, SIMON
HILL, David
Puffin, 1995, ISBN 0 14 036381 5 Pb
Age Interest: Yr.7 - Yr.10   Age Reading: Yr.6+

Nathan has seen Simon going around their small town, firstly on crutches then in a wheel chair. However, they do not go to the same primary school and it is only when they meet up in high school, that they become friends. Simon has muscular dystrophy, but as Nathan says 'once you know him you hardly notice he's in a wheelchair'. Now they are in the fourth form, and Nathan starts to realise that Simon may not be around for much longer. He needs an electric wheelchair, and seems to be spending longer periods in hospital, but this does not stop Simon living life to the full. Simon's final year of life is recounted by his best friend Nathan. Despite this book seeming morbid, it is full of humour and laughter, and Simon is not forgotten by all those with whom he came into contact. Factual information on muscular dystrophy is melded into the story.

116 SEEING OFF UNCLE JACK

ASHLEY, Bernard

Puffin, 1993, ISBN 0 14 034794 1 Pb

Chivers, 1991, ISBN 0 7451 6907 4 Hb Lp

Age Interest: Yr.7 - Yr.10   Age Reading: Yr.7+

Three short stories based in the UK about an Afro-Caribbean family. The title story deals with the death of an uncle. When Uncle Jack dies, twelve-year-old Winnie finds out the truth about her uncle's blindness. He had been a dancer and gone on tour to South Africa. No one had mentioned that he was black when booking, and when he arrived, he got caught up in an anti-apartheid demonstration and was blinded when a gas grenade hit him. Winnie feels very proud at discovering a side of Uncle Jack she never knew.

117 SINK OR SWIM

POTTS, Ghillian

BRAZELL, Derek

Young Corgi, 1993, ISBN 0 552 52753 X Pb

Age Interest: Yr.4 - Yr.6   Age Reading: Yr.3+

Ever since his dad died, William has not mentioned him and has withdrawn into himself. However, when Mark the class bully starts to pick on him and his friends, he decides it is time to stand up for himself. He devises a strategy to stop Mark, but all does not go to plan and one day he is faced with having to save a baby from drowning due to Mark's actions. Though he is scared, William remembers all the things his father taught him, including how to swim and dive, and to take one step at a time. This dramatic rescue is the catalyst for William to come to terms with his father's death, talk about him to his mother and remember all the good times they had together. Dad will always be with William, through the things he taught him.

118 STACY HAD A LITTLE SISTER

FRIEDMAN, Judith

OLD, Wendie C

Albert Whitman, USA, 1995, ISBN 0 8075 7598 4 Hb

Age Interest: Yr.1 - Yr.4   Age Reading: Yr.3+

This is a full and complete account of Sudden Infant Death Syndrome through the eyes of the big sister. It begins with the joy of the birth of the new baby, followed by an account of everyday family life and culminating in the impact of the baby's sudden death. It deals with the feelings of the parents and their effect on Stacy; her sadness, bewilderment and feelings of guilt (was she somehow to blame?). The book illustrates with words and pictures the sadness and grief felt by the whole family. It could be used to help answer many questions from a child in a similar situation.

119 STEVE: A STORY ABOUT DEATH

NEWMAN, Marjorie

Franklin Watts, 1995, ISBN 0 7496 2026 9 Hb

Age Interest: Yr.4 - Yr.7   Age Reading: Yr.5+

A title from the 'Horizons' Series which looks at issues such as Bullying, AIDS, Homelessness and in this case Death, presented in a fiction format. Steve who is eleven and his sister Gemma aged nine, are told one day at school that their father has been involved in an accident and mum has gone to the hospital. A neighbour takes them home, but mum arrives to tell them that dad has died. We follow the family as they try and cope with this horrible situation. Most of the story is told through the eyes of Steve as he tries to sort out his feelings and anger. They visit the building site where dad died, the chapel of rest and see him in the coffin. The following week the funeral takes place and then suddenly there is just the three of them as all the relatives have gone home. Slowly life restarts for them all.

120 STOPPING FOR DEATH: POEMS OF DEATH AND LOSS

DUFFY, Carol Ann ed.

RAFFERTY, Trisha

Viking, 1996, ISBN 0 670 85416 6 Pb

Age Interest: Yr.6+   Age Reading: Yr.5+

An anthology of poems dealing mainly with death, but also touching on other forms of loss - friendship, relationships, time. Contributors include Seamus Heaney, Grace Nichols, Roger McGough, Alice Walker, Charles Causley. A wide range of viewpoints from many cultures, philosophies and religions are included. An eclectic mix of poems which should contain something to which everybody can relate.

121 STRAIGHT TALK ABOUT DEATH FOR TEENAGERS: HOW TO COPE WITH LOSING SOMEONE YOU LOVE

GROLLMAN, Earl A.

Beacon Press, USA, 1993, ISBN 0 8070 2501 1 Pb

Age Interest: Yr.9+   Age Reading: Yr.7+

The author wrote this book in response to teenagers who asked 'How come when someone dies, people forget about us? Everyone is trying to help the little kids or the parents, but what about us? Don't we count?' The author, who has written more than twenty books on death and other crises, presents us with a simply but carefully written book to counsel teenagers, and help them cope and express their feelings after a death, whether it be family member, friend, or classmate. The death of parents, grandparents, siblings, friends, accidental deaths, suicide, AIDS, violent death and terminal illness are all looked at. This is also a book that teenagers could read for themselves.

122 THE SUMMER OF LILY & ESME

QUINN, *John*

Poolbeg Press, Eire, 1991, ISBN 1 85371 162 4 Pb

Age Interest: Yr.7 - Yr.10   Age Reading: Yr.7+

Alan has lived all his life in Dublin and is not looking forward to moving to the country. His nearest neighbours are two elderly ladies (Lily and Esme of the title) which he does not find promising. However, when they start calling him Albert, and he finds this is the name of a boy who died many years ago, a mystery adventure seems in the offing. With his new friend Lisa they set out to solve the mystery of the Albert's death. Through Lily and Esme they find out about life before, during and after World War I, the countless deaths - including Albert's - that occurred, and how they affected so many lives. At the end of the story Lily also dies.

123 SUPPORT AND COUNSELLING FOR GRIEVING FAMILIES

The Child Bereavement Trust

1 Millside, Riversdale, Bourne End, Bucks. SL8 5EB

Age Interest: Adult

This pack contains four booklets and twenty-two double-sided A4 sheets to help families and their carers cope, adapt and come to terms with, the death of a baby or child. The nature of the pack means that relevant information can be taken out and used by or with the parents and family who are grieving. Especially useful are the two booklets *My Book About Me* and *My Book About Our Baby That Died* that will enable children to explore and put down on paper their feelings of grief.

124 TALKING ABOUT DEATH: A DIALOGUE BETWEEN PARENT AND CHILD

GROLLMAN, *Earl A.*

AVISHAI, *Susan*

Beacon Press, USA, 1991, 3rd rev ed. ISBN 0 8070 2363 9 Pb

Age Interest: Adult

How do you explain the death of a loved one to a child? This updated seminal text by a leader in the field of grief counselling in America is for parents and those working with children, who have to face this situation. As every child will come into contact with some form of death as they grow up, this is a book that every adult would find useful reading before such an event occurs. As well as factual information for adults, sections of this book can be shared and used by children as a way of exploring their feelings.

125 THROUGH GRIEF: THE BEREAVEMENT JOURNEY
COLLICK, Elizabeth
Darton, Longman & Todd, 1986, ISBN 0 232 51682 0 Pb
Age Interest: Adult

Written from personal experience after the death of her husband, the author, who is a bereavement counsellor, offers a book that is full of practical good sense, that will be of use to the bereaved as well as to professionals, family and friends. She also takes time to look at 'Life's Little Deaths' - children leaving home, divorce, losing a limb; all of which lead to grieving.

126 TIGER EYES
BLUME, Judy
Heinemann, 1984, ISBN 0 435 12278 9 Hb
Piper, 1988, ISBN 0 330 26954 2 Pb
Age Interest: Yr.6 - Yr.10   Age Reading: Yr.7+

After the brutal murder of her father in his shop in Atlantic City, Davey, her mother and younger brother go to stay with relatives in New Mexico. Though they are now thousands of miles of miles from the scene Davey is still consumed with rage and grief and is unaware that there are other people mourning and suffering. Striking up a friendship with a young man called Wolf, she slowly comes to terms with what happened to her father and is also able to see the pain of her mother and brother. Eventually it is time to move back to Atlantic City but she knows she can't go back to the way it was, 'You have to pick up the pieces and keep moving ahead.'

127 A TIME TO BE BORN
MAYFIELD, Sue
Scholastic, 1995, ISBN 0 590 54188 9 Pb
Age Interest: Yr.7 - Yr.11   Age Reading: Yr.7+

This is the sequel to *I Carried You On Eagle's Wings* (65), reviewed earlier in this handbook. With his GCSEs finished and a long summer ahead of him, Tony is slowly coming to terms with the death of his mother just over a year ago, but still feels very angry and lonely. He also cannot accept that his father seems to have got on with life without any problems, including dating another women. School friendships and his relationship with his friend Clare are changing, all in all a summer for growing up.

128 A TIME TO MOURN: GROWING THROUGH THE GRIEF PROCESS

KAST, Verena

Daimon Books, Switzerland, 1992, ISBN 3 85630 509 2 Pb

Age Interest: Adult

The author is a professor of psychology and a psychotherapist, and this book grew out of her doctoral dissertation. It was originally published in German. She believes that we need to understand grief as it is an important factor in our psychic health. Over many years she has collected and analysed the dreams of people who are grieving; dreams she feels are 'the way in which the unconscious prompts us to deal with mourning'. She looks at the various stages of grief and uses dreams to illustrate this process and to give practical examples from therapeutical work she has carried out with patients.

129 TIMOTHY DUCK: THE STORY OF THE DEATH OF A FRIEND

BLACKBURN, Lynn Bennett

Centering Corporation, USA, 1987, ISBN 1 56123 013 8 Pb

Age Interest: N - Yr.3   Age Reading: Yr.2+

Timothy Duck is a very inquisitive bird, always wanting to know why this or that happens. John a young boy who comes to the pond to feed the ducks, also wants to know the why of everything. They become friends, but as the months pass Timothy notices that John is ill and sometimes doesn't come to the park. He asks his mother why people can't make John better, but she says that sometimes people get so sick that no one can make them better. Eventually John no longer comes to the park and Timothy finds out that he has died. His mother explains what will happen to the body - that there will be a funeral for John's family and friends to say goodbye. Timothy Duck also goes to the funeral to say goodbye, but he is still very sad and angry and another duck who lost a sister explains how she coped with bereavement. A simply told story that could be used as a starting point to explain death to very young children.

130 TOPHER AND THE TIME-TRAVELLING CAT

JARMAN, Julia

Anderson, 1992, ISBN 0 86264 409 7 Hb

HarperCollins, 1993, ISBN 0 00 674634 9 Pb

Age Interest: Yr.6 - Yr.9   Age Reading: Yr.6+

It has been six months since Topher's mum died and his father has become a neatness and routine freak - a place for everything and everything its place. This seems to be his way of trying to control the anguish of his wife's death. Topher's way of controlling his grief is to try and block out the past. However, when a stray cat walks into their lives which Topher names Ka, weird things start to happen. Involved in these adventures is a new friend he has made at school, Ellie, who is deaf. They are magically taken by Ka back in time to ancient Egypt and by experiencing the rituals that surrounded death in Egypt Topher is able to release his mother.

131 TRESPASSERS

COWLEY, Wanda

Mallinson Rendal, New Zealand, 1991, ISBN 0 908606 76 1 Pb

Age Interest: Yr.8 - Yr.11   Age Reading: Yr:7+

After the death of his wife and youngest son, killed by a drunk driver, Mr Fraser takes his daughter Fiona, and remaining son Neil to live in the country. He alienates his new neighbours when he blocks off an access road that leads to their vineyard. Since they produce alcohol, he believes they are just as much to blame for the deaths in his family as the driver of the car. Neil becomes friendly with Sarah the neighbours' daughter and her friend Sean. The three of them try to help Fiona who has become silent and withdrawn since the accident. Matters come to an explosive head when Mr Fraser discovers Fiona at the vineyard and shots are fired.

132 TUNES FOR BEARS TO DANCE TO

CORMIER, Robert

Hamish Hamilton, 1997, ISBN 0 241 13878 7 Hb

Age Interest: Yr.8 - Yr.12   Age Reading: Yr.7+

A complex novel that examines the abuse of power and evil. After the death of his older brother Eddie, Henry and his parents move house. One of his new neighbours is Mr Levine a survivor of Hitler's concentration camps. An unlikely friendship springs up between the two of them, but this is threatened by Henry's bigoted employer Mr Hairston who hates Mr Levine. A rewarding though difficult book to read as Henry realises the evil he fears most is that inside himself, and therefore inside the reader. Throughout the story his grief over his brother's death comes and goes and influences some of the actions he takes.

133 UNDERSTANDING DEATH AND DYING
CATHCART, Fiona
British Institute of Learning Disabilities, 1994,
ISBN 1 873791 06 2 (set) Pb

A set of three booklets aimed at adults with learning problems, their families and the professionals working with them. There is much in them that will also be of relevance and use to children with learning problems and those assisting them. The booklets can be purchased as a set or individually. Bibliographic details and annotations for individual parts of the set can be found (58, 59 & 147).

134 A VERY EASY DEATH
BEAUVOIR, Simone de
Penguin, 1969, ISBN 0 14 018327 2 Pb
Age Interest: Yr.9+   Age Reading: YR.9+

This is a record of the months leading up to the death of the author's mother from cancer. Up until this moment she had always prided herself on controlling her emotions. Now she is faced with a situation that overwhelms her. With great poignancy and honesty Simone de Beauvoir takes the reader with her on this very personal journey

135 THE WEB
HILTON, Nette
MILLARD, Kerry
HarperCollins, 1992, ISBN 0 207 17245 5 Pb
Age Interest: Yr.4 - Yr.7   Age Reading: Yr.4+

Jenny has a wonderful relationship with her great-grandmother, Violet Anne, and loves going to stay with her. There never seems to be a dull moment as she plays outdoors with Misty the possum and Saffron the lizard, while indoors there is the spare room with all its treasures tracing Violet Anne's life. On this visit there is an extra surprise, Sam who is a seven legged spider. His magic webs bring back happy memories for Violet Anne, as she and Jenny both realise that she is not very well. Going into a nursing home is not a happy move for either Violet Anne or Jenny, and sadly Violet dies. However, Sam the spider weaves one last wonderful web which Jenny is able to save thereby preserving the memories of her great-grandmother. The book also looks sensitively at the issue of old age, and the contribution that older people make to society.

136 WESTERN WIND
FOX, Paula
Orion, 1995, ISBN 1 85881 074 4 Pb
Age Interest: Yr.7 - Yr.11   Age Reading: Yr.7+

Sent to stay with her grandmother for the summer against her own wishes, Elizabeth is determined not to enjoy herself. However through befriending a small boy who may have autistic tendencies she slowly comes to love the peace and isolation of the island. It is a great shock to her when her grandmother collapses one day and Elizabeth learns that gran has a serious heart condition. Her idyllic time on the island comes to an abrupt close and she has to face up the reality of her grandmother dying.

137 WHAT DO WE TELL THE CHILDREN: BOOKS TO USE WITH CHILDREN AFFECTED BY ILLNESS AND BEREAVEMENT
PHILIPS, Kerstin
Paediatric AIDS Resource Centre (PARC), Edinburgh Department of Child Life and Health, 20 Sylvan Place, Edinburgh EH9 1UW, 1996,
ISBN 1 900339 01 3 Pb
Age Interest: Adult

This annotated bibliography was commissioned by PARC in response to the growing number of children whose lives are being affected by HIV and AIDS either directly or indirectly. There are two main emphasises to the bibliography - books on death and books on HIV/AIDS. The titles are divided into fiction and non-fiction and then subdivided into those which can be read and used by children and those for adults working with children. The material on HIV/AIDS is a fairly comprehensive listing and is to be welcomed, as this is a subject area in which many people, professional or otherwise are becoming interested.

138 WHAT DO WE THINK ABOUT DEATH?
BRYANT-MOLE, Karen
Wayland, 1998, ISBN 0 7502 2208 5 Hb
Age Interest: N - Yr.5   Age Reading: Yr.2+

Twelve double-page spreads examine topics such as Dying; Growing Old; Death; Long Lives, Short Lives: Funerals, and Missing Someone. Bright colour photographs, with large bold text in simple language, make this a very accessible book for young children to look at and read. It also contains guidance notes for parents and teachers, who wish to use the book with children.

139 WHEN BAD THINGS HAPPEN TO GOOD PEOPLE
KUSHNER, Harold S.
Pan Books, 1982, ISBN 0 330 26827 9 Pb
Age Interest: Adult

Though this book has been written from the perspective of the Jewish tradition and faith, there is much in it that will be relevant to other religions. The underlying sentiments are common to everyone - why did the person die, what am I going to do now, how can I cope, why did God do this. The author, a Rabbi in America, wrote the book after the death of his son and it is a personal restatement of his belief in God even in the face of tragedy.

140 WHEN MOURNING COMES: A BOOK OF COMFORT FOR THE GRIEVING
SILVERMAN, William B & CINNAMON, Kenneth
Kuperard/Jason Aronson, 1995, ISBN 0 87668 820 2 Hb
Age Interest: Adult

The newly bereaved can feel overwhelmed by feelings of loneliness, loss, isolation and depression. A Rabbi and a clinical psychologist have written this book as a guide to grieving. Having worked with bereaved people for many years and also been through the grieving process themselves, they have a clear insight into grief and bereavement. Here they present practical suggestions to help, not just the person directly affected, but also the family, friends and professionals working with them.

141 WHEN OUR BABY DIED: A VIDEO ABOUT GRIEF FOR PARENTS AND FAMILIES
Surrey Media Services
Professional Care Productions,
1 Millside, Riversdale, Bourne End, Bucks SL8 5EB,
ISBN 0 9521661 3 5 Video
Age Interest: Adult

This is a companion publication to *Grieving After the Death of Your Baby* (57), reviewed earlier in this handbook. Parents, children and grandparents talk about their feelings after the death of a baby in the family. They explain what the death of their baby has meant to them and how it has changed their lives, and they describe some of the things they have done to express their grief, mourn for their baby, and find support for themselves.

142 WHEN SOMEONE VERY SPECIAL DIES: CHILDREN CAN LEARN TO COPE WITH GRIEF

HEEGARD, Marge

Fairview Press, USA, 1991, ISBN 0 9620502 0 2 Pb

Age Interest: Yr.1+   Age Reading: Yr.3+

A book for children with or without learning problems and for adults with learning problems, to record their feelings and emotions as they experience and come to terms with the death of a pet, relative or friend. One page reads: Someone I loved died. This is a picture of that person. (NAME) was important to me because...... There is room to put a picture of the person, insert their name and then write about them. For younger children, the use of drawings can be a valuable outlet for expressing emotions which they may not be able to express verbally or in writing.

143 WHEN SOMETHING TERRIBLE HAPPENS: CHILDREN CAN LEARN TO COPE WITH GRIEF

HEEGARD, Marge

Fairview Press, USA, 1991, ISBN 0 9620502 3 7 Pb

Age Interest: Yr.1+   Age Reading: Yr.2+

Grief is not only felt when someone loved dies, but also as a result of divorce, people moving house, accidents. This booklet will allow children and also adults with learning problems to express their emotions. Pertinent questions and statements appear on each page with space for the child or adult to draw or express their emotions. Drawings are very useful for young children or those who have trouble expressing themselves verbally or in writing, and can be a more expressive way into a person's thought processes.

144 WHEN THE PHONE RANG

MAZER, Harry

Scholastic, USA, 1985, ISBN 0 590 44773 4 Pb

Age Interest: Yr.7 - Yr.10   Age Reading: Yr.7+

Sixteen-year-old Billy lives with his parents and younger sister Lori. Older brother Kevin is away at college. On the day that their parents are due home from a Caribbean holiday, the phone rings and Billy is informed that the plane carrying their parents exploded in mid-air and there are no survivors. At first the children think this is a sick joke, but when they watch the news and see the accident reported, the reality of the situation starts to sink in. It is many days before they can accept that their parents are dead. They have no bodies to bury, so part of the mourning process is denied them. How the three young adults come to terms with their loss is sympathetically explored.

145 WIDOW'S JOURNEY: A RETURN TO LIVING

ROSE, Xenia

Souvenir Press, 1992, ISBN 0 285 65097 1 Hb

Souvenir Press, 1995, ISBN 0 285 65098 X Pb

Age Interest: Adult

'Coming through the grief and pain of losing a loved partner is one of the hardest and most stressful experiences any of us can face. Only those who have been through it can understand just what it means.' The author, a psychotherapist whose husband died of cancer, is therefore in a position to examine the issues surrounding the death of a partner. Without self pity, she talks about the problems and frustrations of acknowledging the reality of her position and is able to give ideas and suggestions for others who might be in the same position.

146 WISH YOU WERE HERE

ZOLOTOW, Charlotte

VENUS, Pamela

BBC Books, 1991, ISBN 0 563 34748 1 Pb.

Age Interest: Yr.2 - Yr.5   Age Reading: Yr.3+

Two stories of loss. The first tells of an unnamed girl whose best friend has moved away. She remembers all the things that they did together at home and at school and wishes she hadn't moved away. The second story is about Lewis who is six. One night he wakes up with a nightmare and his mother comforts him. Lewis says he misses his grandpa, but his mum can't believe he remembers him as Lewis was only two when he died. However, Lewis does remember grandpa and is able to describe him and some of the things they did together. Mum says that grandpa lived a long way from them and because Lewis never mentioned him, she never told him grandpa had died. Mum then tells Lewis of some of the things she remembers about him. Both are comforted by their memories.

147 YOUR FEELINGS

CATHCART, Fiona

British Institute of Learning Disabilities, 1994,

ISBN 1 873791 11 9 Pb

Age Interest: Yr.1+   Age Reading: Yr.3+

This is Booklet 1 from the series 'Understanding Death and Dying', aimed at adults with learning problems, their families and professionals working with them. It contains much that will also be of relevance and use to children with learning problems and those assisting them. This book starts by looking at loss in its widest sense - losing belongings, a friend or relative moving away, and how we might feel about this - sadness, anger, blaming someone else. It then moves on to talk about death - it is an end of living, the person or animal no longer breathes, they cannot hear, see or feel anything. People and animals die because they are old, because of an illness or accident. The dead person can be buried or cremated at a special service called a funeral. Finally emotions and feelings that the bereaved may experience are explored. Reviews of Booklets 2 & 3 are at entries (58 & 59).

AUTHOR INDEX

Numbers refer to the individual entry numbers, not the page numbers

ALDERSON, Priscilla 113

ALLAN, Nicholas 60

ARENA, Felice 33

ASHLEY, Bernard 116

BAILEY, Ann 107

BEAUVOIR, Simone de 134

BERTOIA, Judi 34

BLACKBURN, Lynn Bennett 129

BLUME, Judy 126

BO, Arno 68

BOWKER, John 86

BOWLER, Tim 110

BRYANT-MOLE, Karen 25, 138

BUCKMAN, Dr. Robert 66

BYARS, Betsy 49

CATHCART, Fiona 58, 59, 133, 147

CHALKFACE PROJECT 26

CHAMBERS, Aidan 21

CHICK, Sandra 69

CHILD BEREAVEMENT TRUST 123

CLARK, David 23

COHN, Janice 91

COLLICK, Elizabeth 125

COLLIER, James Lincoln 92

CONRAD, Pam 93

CORMIER, Robert 132

COWLEY, Wanda 131

CRAVEN, Margaret 67

CREW, Gary 84

DEAN, Anna 88

DICK, Harold M 37

DOKA, Kenneth J 13

DUFFY, Carol Ann 120

DUFFY, Wendy 12

DUNLOP, Eileen 53

EHRLICH, Amy 22

ENDE, Michael 99

FENDER, Kay 96

FOX, Paula 136

FRASER, Christine Marion 9

FRIEDMAN, Judith 118

FULLER, Jill 73

GATLIFFE, Eleanor D 29

GREEN, Gerard 17

GROLLMAN, Earl A 41, 80, 121, 124

GUY, Rosa 47

HARPER, Anita 105

HASTINGS, Selina 85

HATFIELD, Jim 24

HEEGARD, Marge 142, 143

HEY, Valerie 64

HILL, David 115

HILL, Susan 71

HILTON, Nette 135

HINTON, John 36

HOLLAND, Cannon Henry Scott 31

HOWARTH, Lesley 43

HUBERT, Cam 35

HUBNER, Franz 52

ISHERWOOD, Sheila 94

JARMAN, Julia 130

JEWETT, Claudia 63

JOBLING, Brenda 102

JONES, Mary 114

JORDAN, Sherryl 100

JORDON, Mary Kate 82

KAST, Verna 128

KATZ, Jeanne 38

KAY, Alan A 72

KEMP, Gene 32

KLEIN, Norma 48

KOHNER, Nancy 57

KROLL, Virginia 61

KUBLER-ROSS, Elisabeth 97

KUSHNER, Harold S 139

KUSUGAK, Michael Arvaarluk 95

L'ENGLE, Madeleine 87, 109

LANTON, Sandy 20

LARSON, Dale G 62

LEACH, Bernadette 70

LEAMAN, Oliver 28

LEAVY, Ina 50

LEWIS, C S 56

LITTLEWOOD, Jane 5

LOHANS, Alison 44

LUBEN, Jacquelynn 19

MAHON, Kate 74

MAHY, Margaret 89

MARRIS, Peter 83

MARTIN, Ann M 75

MAYFIELD, Sue 65, 127

MAZER, Harry 144

MAZZIO, Joann 98

McGOUGH, Roger 76

NEWMAN, Marjorie 119

O'BRINE, Rory 90

PATERSON, Katherine 42

PECK, Rosalie 77

PENNELS, Sister Margaret 45

PERKINS, Ginny 106

PHILIPS, Kerstin 137

POTTS, Ghillian 117

QUINN, John 122

RANDO, Therese 55, 101

RICHARDSON, Jean 30

ROSE, Xenia 145

ROSENBERG, Liz 11

RUSHTON, Lucy 27

SAUNDERS, Cicely 8

SCOTT, Donald 18

SHAWE, Marilyn 40

SILVERMAN, William B 140

SIMMONDS, Posy 46

SIMON, Norma 111

SMITH, Fraser 78

SPELMAN, Cornelia 2

SPURRIER, Libby 3

ST CATHERINE'S HOSPICE 14

STANLEY, Elizabeth 15

STAUDACHER, Carol 7

STEIN, Sara Bonnett 1

STRACHAN, Ian 10

SURREY MEDIA SEVICES 141

THOMPSON, Colin 81

URE, Jean 103

VARLEY, Susan 6

VIGNA, Judith 112

WADDELL, Martin 51, 79

WALKER, Richard 108

WALLBANK, Susan 39

WESTALL, Robert 104

WHITAKER, Agnes 4

WOJCIECHOWSKI, Susan 16

WORDEN, J William 54

ZOLOTOW, Charlotte 146

KEYWORD INDEX

In order to simplify the use of this handbook all entries are arranged alphabetically by title in the main section, with every entry being given an individual number. This index allows the user to find a specific topic and go direct to the relevant numbered entries.

ACCIDENTAL DEATH 21, 33, 44, 49, 67, 68, 87, 89, 93, 98, 111, 112, 119, 131, 144

ANTHOLOGIES 4, 8, 31, 40, 72, 78, 120

BIBLIOGRAPHIES 137

COUNSELLING 3, 5, 7, 12, 13, 17, 18, 19, 23, 30, 34, 36, 37, 38, 39, 45, 54, 55, 62, 63, 66, 72, 77, 80, 83, 97, 101, 114, 121, 123, 125, 128, 140, 145

DEATH OF A:

Child
10, 16, 37, 40, 76, 101, 111, 123, 131

Friend
6, 9, 10, 21, 87, 96, 98, 103, 104, 109, 115, 122, 129

Grandparent
1, 48, 50, 51, 52, 81, 94, 110, 111, 135, 136, 146

Husband/Wife/Partner
16, 33, 39, 56, 71, 114, 125, 130, 131, 145

Infant (*Neo & Ante Natal*)
19, 57, 64, 91, 101, 105, 113, 118, 123, 141

Other Relative
49, 82, 93, 111, 116

Parent
2, 11, 20, 22, 33, 42, 44, 47, 65, 68, 69, 70, 73, 74, 77, 79, 95, 100, 102, 107, 112, 117, 119, 126, 127, 130, 131, 134, 144

	Pet 1, 15, 32, 46, 60, 61, 75
	Sibling 44, 53, 84, 88, 89, 92, 93, 105, 106, 107, 131, 132
DEATH PRACTICES	**Burial** 25, 26, 27, 147
	Cremation 25, 26, 27, 147
	Religious Observations 20, 23, 25, 27, 41, 72, 78, 86, 139
EXPLAINING DEATH	1, 12, 14, 20, 24, 25, 26, 27, 28, 29, 30, 41, 45, 58, 59, 108, 121, 124, 133, 137, 138, 142, 147
MEMORY BOOKS	90, 123, 142, 143
PHILOSOPHY OF DEATH	43, 67, 85, 99, 122
SUICIDE	17, 18, 35, 103
TERMINAL ILLNESS	**AIDS** 3, 82
	Cancer *(including Leukaemia)* 9, 20, 34, 44, 47, 65, 67, 109, 114, 127, 134, 145
	Heart Attack/Disease 73, 136
	Other 10, 100, 115
VIOLENT DEATH	**Murder** 74, 126
	War or Civil Disturbance 92

ORGANISATIONS AND THEIR ADDRESSES

These organisations offer help and advice to those caring for children who are suffering from a life-threatening condition, and people who have been bereaved and are grieving. Most organisations have printed leaflets available. When writing for information it is best to enclose a stamped self-addressed envelope.

ACTION FOR SICK CHILDREN,
(Formerly NAWCH)
First Floor, 300 Kingston Road,
Wimbledon, London SW20 8LX
Tel: 0181 542 4848
E-mail:
action_for_sick_children_edu@msm.com
Website:
http://www.actionforsickchildren.org.uk
Works for the welfare of children in hospital.

ACT
65 St. Michael's Hill, Bristol BS2 8DZ
Tel: 0117 922 1556
Help for families whose children have life-threatening and terminal conditions.

ALDER CENTRE
Royal Liverpool Children's NHS Trust
Alder Hey, Eaton Road,
Liverpool L12 2AP
Tel: 0151 252 5391
Tel: 0800 282986
(Helpline: Monday to Sunday 7pm - 10pm; Monday, Wednesday, Friday 10am - 1pm)
Provides a range of services, including counselling, groups, befriending for parents and professionals affected by the death of a child. Also offers a training and consultancy service. See also entry for **Child Death Helpline**.

BARNARDO'S
Tanners Lane, Barkingside, Ilford,
Essex IG6 1QG
Tel: 0181 550 8822
E-mail: barninfo@compuserve.com
Website: http://barnardos.org.uk
Barnardo's is the largest child care charity in the UK, with 300 projects providing for the needs of 30,000 children and their families. Many of these projects serve children who have experienced or are expected to experience bereavement, such as through a parent or carer contracting AIDS. Other projects provide counselling and support for parents and carers of children who have died following a disability or terminal illness.

BRITISH ASSOCIATION FOR COUNSELLING
BAC, 1 Regent Close, Rugby,
Warwickshire CV21 3PJ
Tel: 01788 578328
Will give advice, support & counselling.

CANCERBACUP
3 Bath Place, Rivington Street,
London EC2A 3DR
Tel: 0171 613 2121
(Information Line)
Tel: 0171 696 9003 (Administration)
For information on cancer and caring for a patient with cancer.

CANCER AND LEUKEMIA IN CHILDHOOD TRUST (CLIC)

CLIC Headquarters, 12-13 King Square, Bristol BS2 8JH
Tel: 0117 924 8844
Support through hands-on nursing care; support with homes-from-homes; invests in research projects for possible cures.

CHILD DEATH HELPLINE

Great Ormond Street Hospital, Great Ormond Street, London WC1N 3JH
Tel: 0800 282986 (Evenings 7pm - 10pm, & Monday, Wednesday and Friday mornings 10am - 1pm)
The Helpline provides a confidential, nation-wide service for anyone affected by the death of a child of any age, at any time, under any circumstances. See also entry for the Alder Centre.

THE COMPASSIONATE FRIENDS

53 North Street, Bristol BS3 1EN
Tel: 0117 966 5202 (Administration)
Tel: 0117 953 9639 (Helpline)
Support for bereaved parents and their immediate families by those similarly bereaved.

CRUSE

Cruse House, 126 Sheen Road, Richmond, Surrey TW9 1UR
Tel: 0181 940 4818
Tel: 0181 332 7227 (Helpline)
Provides support and help for all bereaved persons. Nearly 200 local branches offering counselling and information to the bereaved. Wide range of publications available.

DEPARTMENT OF SOCIAL SECURITY

Leaflets Unit, PO Box 21, Stanmore, Middlesex HA7 1AY
Provides various guides.

FOUNDATION FOR THE STUDY OF INFANT DEATHS

14 Halkin Street, London SW1X 7DP
Tel: 0171 235 1721 (Helpline)
Tel: 0171 235 0965 (General Enquiries)
E-mail: fsid@sids.org.uk
Website:
http://www.sids.org.uk/fsid/
FSID, founded in 1971, is the UK's leading cot death organisation. It aims to prevent infant deaths and promote health, and it carries out its aims by funding research (over £7m to date), supporting bereaved families and disseminating information about infant death and infant care to health professionals and the public.

GOOD GRIEF

Barbara Ward, 3 Wheelwright Court, Walkhampton, Yelverton, Devon PL20 6LA
Runs courses on counselling and learning about bereavement. Aimed at parents, teachers, carers and children. Barbara Ward is also the author of the two teaching packs - Good Grief 1 for under elevens, and Good Grief 2 for over elevens and adults.

JEWISH BEREAVEMENT COUNSELLING SERVICE

PO Box 6748, London N3 3BX
Tel: 0181 349 0839
Counselling and support for all who have been bereaved. Provided by trained voluntry counsellors, who are professionally supervised. London area only.

LESBIAN AND GAY BEREAVEMENT PROJECT

Vaughn M Williams Centre,
Colindale Hospital, Colindale Avenue,
London NW9 5HG
Tel: 0181 200 0511
(Monday - Thursday 11am - 6pm)
Tel: 0181 455 8894
(Helpline, 7pm - 12pm)
Support to bereaved lesbian and gay people, or anyone bereaved by the death of a lesbian or gay person.

MACMILLAN CANCER RELIEF

Anchor House, 15-19 Britten Street,
London SW3 3TZ
Tel: 0171 351 7811
Tel: 0845 601 6161
    (Information Line)
Provides expert treatment and care through specialist Macmillan nurses, doctors, and buildings for cancer treatment and care.

NATIONAL ASSOCIATION OF BEREAVEMENT SERVICES

20 Norton Folgate, Bishopsgate,
London E1 6DB
Tel: 0171 247 0617
Tel: 0171 247 1080 (Helpline - open Weekdays 10am to 4pm. Outside these hours an answer machine is in operation)
Umbrella organisation for all bereavement organisations. Acts as a referral agency by putting bereaved and grieving people in touch with their nearest local service.

THE NATIONAL SOCIETY (CHURCH OF ENGLAND) FOR PROMOTING RELIGIOUS EDUCATION

Church House, Great Smith Street,
London SW1P 3NZ
Tel: 0171 222 1672
E-mail: info@natsoc.org.uk
Website: http://www.natsoc.org.uk
Provides advice, information and publications on a wide range of topics, including death and bereavement.

NATURAL DEATH CENTRE

20 Heber Road, London NW2 6AA
Tel: 0181 208 2853
Website: http://www.globalideasbank.org/naturaldeath.html
Provides a befriending network of volunteers to sit with those who are critically ill, to relieve carers. Also provides advice on environmentally friendly and inexpensive funerals.

ROYAL SOCIETY FOR MENTALLY HANDICAPPED CHILDREN AND ADULTS (MENCAP)
123 Golden Lane, London EC1 0RT
Tel: 0171 454 0454

ST. CHRISTOPHER'S HOSPICE
Halley Stewart Library,
51-59 Lawrie Park Road, Sydenham,
London SE26 6DZ
Tel: 0181 778 9252
The library contains a specialised, multidisciplinary collection of literature on care of the terminally ill, and bereavement.

SAMARITANS
Head Office, 10 The Grove, Slough,
Berkshire SL1 1QP
Tel: 0345 909090
The Samaritans work 24 hours a day, 365 days a year, supporting any person who is in despair.

SANDS
Still Birth and Neonatal Death Society
28 Portland Place, London W1N 4DE
Tel: 0171 436 7940
Tel: 0171 436 5881
(Helpline   9.30am - 5pm
                 Monday - Friday)
Offers support for bereaved parents that have had a still birth or neonatal death. Over 200 local groups throughout the UK. Guidelines for Health Care Professionals working with bereaved parents and their families.

TERRENCE HIGGINS TRUST
52-54 Grays Inn Road,
London WC1X 8JU
Tel: 0171 831 0330
E-Mail: info@tht.org.uk
Website: http://www.tht.org.uk
For all information on caring for people with HIV.

TAMBA
PO Box 30, Little Sutton,
South Wirral L66 1TH
Tel: 0151 348 0020
Tel: 01732 868000 (Helpline)
Gives support to families who have lost one or more of twins or a higher multiple set.

YAD B YAD
Tel: 0181 444 7134
E-Mail: heilbron@cheerful.com
Jewish children grief and bereavement project. Provides resource information, booklists and training services for professionals working with bereaved children.